MURDER AT THEATRE X

A NOVEL BY
CHRISTINA SQUIRE

Copyright ©2018 by Christina Squire

Cover concept by Charles Squire

Cover design by George Paloheimo Jr.

ABQ Press Trade Paper Edition 2018

www.abqpress.com

Albuquerque, New Mexico

ISBN 978-1-64316-759-6

Acknowledgements

My thanks and deepest appreciation go to Lynn C. Miller
and the members of her writing critique group:
Lynda Miller, Laurie Hause, Tina Carlson,
Kim Feldman and Jill Root.

Thanks to my publisher Judith Van Gieson
for her support and encouragement.

I also want to thank Patricia Carpenter,
Dr. Wilbur Williams, and Scott George
of the UNM Recycling Center.

I have worked and gotten an advanced degree from the
UNM Department of Theatre and Dance. I knew many
wonderful, talented people. Characters in this book are
dramatic creations and pure fiction.

Chapter 1

"Swimming through velvet."

"What?" my sister said.

"Swimming through velvet! You heard me!" I said. I put both hands around my martini glass as if in prayer. We were sitting on high stools at our favorite round table in the window of Scalo's *il Bar*.

"So cousin Julie told you how our Mom described having sex with Dad, too?"

"On my wedding day driving to the church."

"Oh, please! When she told me that on my wedding day, I laughed 'til I cried. Julie patted me on the back, told me not to worry, and that everything was going to be all right eventually!"

"She was trying to be helpful, but I have never erased the visual of our parents having sex from my mind's eye!"

"Amen, sister! I think Julie was trying to prepare us for our wedding night, so we wouldn't be afraid. She thought we were virgins."

Sally and I burst out laughing so loudly that people turned their heads.

"In spite of all the Macedonian guilt pounded into us growing up, we still had sex before marriage. Ruined! We were whores!" Sally clinked my glass. "To us *kurvas.*"

"But, Sally, I finally swam through velvet with James...," I whispered.

"Tell me everything." Sally leaned her head close to mine.

I started to cry. I dabbed my eyes with a napkin. People stared at us again. Laughing and crying...the Macedonian way. No, we needed some screaming, too, but this was not the place.

Sally held my hand. "Oh Caro! You don't have to go into detail! Velvet says it all!"

I wanted to laugh, but just hiccupped.

"So," she said, "you had a moment with James."

I nodded. "Several...," I said.

"OK, a few. And no one was hurt, and you still have people here who love you, and life will go on..."

"He went back to New Orleans."

"And you are here and will remember Abiquiu forever—"

"And Santa Fe."

"What?" Sally dropped my hand. She drained her martini.

"Well...we were driving back to Albuquerque so he could catch his plane and, well, he said that he had never been to Santa Fe, so I pulled off the highway into the City Different and ended up somehow at Las Palomas Inn and..."

"You went swimming again."

We both flagged the waiter at the same time and held up our empty glass.

"And an order of fried calamari and some bread, please," I said.

"Have you heard from James since he left?" Sally asked.

"No."

"Oh Caro...I don't know what to say."

"There's nothing to say. Just be happy for me."

"I don't want you hurt."

"Inconceivable, Sally."

I, Caroline Steele, married twenty years, mother of three, secretary, amateur sleuth, was going to Hell. Or not. (My fellow Episcopalians ignored the fiery depths.) After helping solve two murders at the University of New Mexico Observatory and the campus Art Museum with James Hutchinson, Inspector in the New Orleans Police Force on temporary assignment in Albuquerque, I finally fell into his heavenly embrace. I earned a big red A on my chest. But I had no regrets. James had awakened the passionate spirit within me. Life was different now. Just how different I had yet to discover.

Christina Squire

Chapter 2

I saw my husband John standing in the front yard watering the grass when I drove in from Abiquiu, New Mexico. James and I had been at the Georgia O'Keeffe Foundation's Appreciation Banquet held in the small town where the famous artist had lived. We were invited since we had discovered that two works of O'Keeffe's art in the University of New Mexico Art Museum were copies while trying to solve a murder. Accountants traced the money trail of millions of dollars paid for the originals to the bank account of the seller: the director of the art museum. The buyer returned the originals to the university.

"You're late. I was worried." John gave me a bear hug. "Did you have a good time?" He put his arm around me as we walked into the house.

"Yes. Everyone was so kind. There was a delicious dinner last night. The tour today of Georgia O'Keeffe's home took longer than I thought. Then I had a late lunch at the Abiquiu Inn with some museum staff. Beautiful day!"

"Was that Inspector there?"

"Yes." I bent down to pet my dog Suki who was whining for attention. "Where are the boys?"

"Douglas has a gig at the Gruet Winery. Max is…I don't know…"

Max opened his bedroom door. "I'm here." He walked up to me. "Mom."

"Max."

We hugged each other tightly.

"Did you have fun?" he asked.

"Yes."

"You both are acting like you haven't seen each other for weeks instead of two days," John said.

"You're on linear time, Dad. In social studies class we are studying the Aboriginal concept of circular and dream time." John and I stared at him. "Very interesting. I have been in circle time about my priorities lately." Max went back into his room. He turned around. "You've probably been on dream time, Mom." He closed the door.

He knew, I thought.

"What priorities," John muttered. "Smoking pot is his only one…Never heard of dream time."

"I think it was the beginning of knowledge in Aboriginal mythology. Or something…"

"Sounds new age. So did you gain any knowledge in Abiquiu?"

"Georgia's house was boring."

"OK. So much for knowledge. Hungry? I made dinner," he said.

"Chinese food?"

"God, no!" He laughed remembering the recent

dinner he made that involved exploding oil and a cast of thousand vegetables. "I grilled chicken and opened a bag salad. Oh…And Peter called from Austin. He's fully recovered his strength from having mono. He said he was working hard finishing the incomplete grades for credit. I can't believe our number one will be a junior at The University of Texas. Where has the time gone, honey?"

"I don't know, John."

"And…guess what came?" He picked up an envelope from the dining room table. "From the UNM Office of Graduate Studies."

I laughed. "I forgot that I applied to the Theatre and Dance Grad Program!"

"You've been busy," John said.

In a rush to get a job at the University Art Museum and possibly run into my Inspector who was investigating another campus murder, I had forgotten the other options I lined up for myself: renewing my secondary school teaching license and applying to graduate school in theatre. Acting was my passion. (Aside from my children.) (And my Inspector.)

I opened the envelope. "I've been accepted!"

John hugged me. "Now you can do what you've loved ever since high school! And you can quit that torture job at the Art Museum."

"It's not that bad, but…I have to process all this, John. In hydrotherapy."

"Enjoy! And congratulations, Caro." He gave me a juicy kiss. He was being very sweet. But I wondered if he and Alice, his secretary at his CPA firm, continued their relationship. If there even was one. I had only seen them out to lunch, a few texts from her when he left his phone in the den, and some mysterious "emergency audits" where John had to stay overnight in different cities.

I certainly had no right to judge.

Chapter 3

I sunk into a lobster bath. I was mentally turning in a circular time of my life: security, passion, the future, responsibility and doubt. What were my priorities? Did I want to go to graduate school? What else did I have to do? There were no guarantees I would see James again. He was married. I was married. We had moments. I had never experienced such moments.

But I always felt alive on stage. Like I felt with James. Theatre was make-believe. Playing. Were James and I just playing? No history or responsibilities together. Like a play, were we ephemeral? Transitory? Fleeting?

Will I suffer the consequences of my actions?

Will my youngest child betray me? As I sank up to my neck in the fragrant water, I thought about the times Max had mysteriously appeared out of nowhere when James and I were close. I wouldn't be surprised if he skipped school and asked one of his older twitty friends to drive him up to Abiquiu. That boy will do me in yet.

Christina Squire

But my fears were not reality. For now I relived my Inspector's farewell kisses in the airport parking structure, the airport elevator, and the airport security line.

People stared.

Chapter 4

I walked into the kitchen the next morning to find Max standing at the counter making a burrito. Grated cheese, chopped onion and strips of green chili were piled on the cutting board. He was carefully layering leftover chicken on top of a flour tortilla. He did not turn around.

I poured him some orange juice. I put some cream in a cup and zapped it in the microwave before adding coffee. I sprayed ReddiWip on top. Max opened his mouth while layering the cheese and chili on top of the chicken. I sprayed some in. Suki pranced around my feet. I sprayed some in her mouth.

Silence.

I opened the *Albuquerque Journal.* I removed the advertisements for Max to read.

Silence.

"So did Dad and Douglas get off OK?" I asked.

"Yes." Max slid his creation into the microwave.

"Back to the Art Museum salt mines for me," I said.

Silence. This was bad, I thought.

"You should go to graduate school, Mom."

I perked up. "Really? You think so? I'm ready for something new."

Silence. Max did not look at me.

"So the Inspector was in Abiquiu?" He stared out the kitchen window as he ran water over a knife.

"Yes."

"All the way from New Orleans?" He put the knife in the dishwasher and started wiping off the counter tops.

Oh he was acting weird!

"Yes," I said.

"That's nice." The microwave pinged. Max rolled his tortilla up, plopped spoonfuls of sour cream on top, sat down, and flipped through the newspaper ads. "He drove there?" He took a huge bite.

He still did not make eye contact.

"No, he flew."

"Into the Santa Fe airport? Rented a car?"

I was tired of twenty-one questions! He probably knew everything anyway. "No! Albuquerque. I picked him up, and we drove to Abiquiu together."

"And he flew back?"

"Yes, he flew back, Max."

"And you're back, Mom!" He jumped up, ran around the table and kissed me. I felt warm cheese and sour cream on my cheek. A wonderful feeling.

"Thank you, Max." My eyes filled with tears.

Chapter 5

I walked Suki to Hidden Park. I loved this oasis located in the middle of a neighborhood block enclosed by the fenced back yards of houses. The big trees and lush grass always calmed me. I entered through a narrow vine-covered alley. Like I was going into another world. I sat on a bench and watched a group practicing Tai Chi. Suki lay down at my feet.

What was I going to do? I went over my options. I did not have to keep working at the Art Museum. My favorite co-worker, Pat, left. Not to mention my Inspector. I had to get real about our relationship. He made no promises and neither did I. I could leave John. My marriage was calm. Very calm. John and I were like brother and sister sharing a house and supporting our family together. Nothing more, which was fine with me most of the time. I was no red hot momma. And John seemed distracted. I wondered why. Sometimes.

But I had to do something. I was full. Of something. Yet hungry. For something.

Suki was getting restless. I got up to walk her around the park. One woman who was practicing Tai Chi ran

13

away from the group. A young man broke off chasing her. They raced around trees laughing. She stopped. He caught up to her. They embraced and kissed. I knew their joy.

In an interview Peruvian writer Mario Vargas Llosa spoke about *amour fou*, the French concept of crazy love: It enriched people, gave them illusions, a kind of appetite for life. I experienced *amour fou* with James. If our time was indeed an illusion, I was still stronger for it. I will go forward.

Chapter 6

I gave notice at the Art Museum. I was only sorry to leave my three student helpers. They were such bright spots while I worked in that mausoleum. The museum administrators accepted my resignation. They were rather cool but oddly happy for me. First real emotions I ever saw them express. I imagined they were exhausted from all the drama in their sealed domain and relieved that I was going to take my theatrics on stage. My son Douglas, who was a freshman at the university, will not be eligible for a tuition waiver anymore, but his father could afford it.

I brought my acceptance letter in person to the Theatre and Dance Office. I waited and waited for Clarence, the Administrative Assistant, to acknowledge my presence. He wore a purple paisley shirt and sharply creased black pants. His short, shiny dark hair had a knife sharp center part. His beautifully manicured fingers flew over the keyboard. I cleared my throat. Finally Clarence swiveled away from his computer screen.

"Well if it isn't Miss Marple," he said.

15

I laughed remembering when my Inspector and I watched him crack open a locker in the Theatre dressing room which revealed an important clue to the murder in the art museum. "Hi, Clarence. How are you?"

"Miserable, as usual. What's the buzz?"

"I've been accepted to graduate school." I handed him my letter of acceptance.

"Are you crazy, girlfriend? Well, you'll fit right in this place." He tossed my letter in the Chair's mailbox. Then he sashayed around his desk and gave me a hug. He smelled so good. "Good luck. You'll need it."

Great, I thought. Another dysfunctional university hotbed of intrigue. I should go back to middle school. Teaching was the ultimate acting job, after all.

Chapter 7

The following week I received an e-mail from Professor Richard Smith. He was going to be my grad advisor and wanted to meet with me the next day. Years before I had taken both semesters of History of Film and Media and Social Change from him. He had a joint position in the Cinematic Arts and Theatre Departments. He was an excellent teacher. I looked forward to seeing him again.

His office was in the basement of the Fine Arts Center down the hall from Theatre X, the department's Black Box performance space. His door was closed. I started to knock when I heard a shrill female voice screaming and a low, basso voice talking. Wow. Drama. I leaned against the wall and waited. The door opened with such force it crashed into the wall. A pretty young woman came out dressed in a long red skirt and black and white polka dot blouse. Mascara ran down her tear-stained face. Her blonde hair fell wildly out of the bun at the base of her neck.

"He's the devil," she hissed to me in a heavy Spanish accent. Then yelled "*Diablo*" as she ran down the hall waving her hands.

Oh my God, I thought. The temperature just rose in this hotbed of intrigue.

"Please come in, Caroline," Richard said. "Have a seat."

I sat in front of his desk. I looked at the walls covered with movie posters: *Sex, Lies and Video Tape, Last Tango in Paris, Secretary*. I looked at him. Richard was a thin, tall, late middle-aged man. He sported a greasy comb over of thin dark hair and his piercing blue eyes constantly blinked. He looked different than he did teaching behind a podium. Not distinguished anymore. Now he looked like a spent Satyr.

"Sorry you had to witness that," Richard said smoothly. "Foreign students come here and expect special treatment. And she's a Flamenco dancer." He winked at me. "Well, you know dancers."

"What about dancers?" I asked.

"Not very bright. Not prepared for graduate level academic courses. All that reading and writing. They think they can just dance their way through grad school..."

"I took dance classes for years here. There were all kinds of academic women who danced with me—"

"We have to talk about your program, Caro." He picked up my file.

"OK."

"This fall you will be Professor Sam Block's teaching assistant for Theatre Appreciation. I assigned you to him because of your acting background in community theatre, your experience as a stage manager, and your teaching credentials. And last but not least, your excellent grades in English classes, and you can write."

"Thank you," I said.

He read through my creative resume. "I see you've done some film work."

"Why, yes…"

"What kind? I can't tell by the titles." He rolled his chair away from his desk and faced me. His eyes started twinkling. Our knees were almost touching. I felt heat coming off of him…like he was ready to pounce.

"Oh two student productions…a Public Service Announcement for drunk driving, a film for the NM Realtors, and a few independent—"

"Did you enjoy acting in independent movies?"

"Yes."

"What did you play?"

"A chain smoking secretary, a crazy mother, a socialite—"

"Love interests?"

"Oh no!"

"Shame. You need to be in a film with one! You are so pretty…Red hair…hazel eyes. And you have womanly curves." He started blinking rapidly.

Silence. I suddenly wanted to run out of there.

"I'm surprised, Caro." Richard rolled back around to face his desk. "You should pick your roles more carefully. If you are comfortable in your skin, you could make a lot of money."

"I'll keep that in mind, Professor Smith," I lied. What a creep. He made my skin crawl. I wished I could have picked another advisor. Maybe I still can.

Richard waved his hand in the air. "Good girl! Now! Where were we?" He assumed a professorial tone. "You

19

will be my assistant director in the Spring for *An Ideal Husband,* and you will direct two Irish Plays for the Campus wide Irish Renaissance next year, and this fall we are presenting an Evening of Beckett Short Plays. You will direct one. And you will register for twelve hours of classwork, of course."

"Of course."

Richard shuffled my transcripts. "You have earned a number of graduate credit hours in English beyond your bachelor's degree—"

"I love to read—"

"You have to get out of your head to succeed here, Caro."

"I'll try, Professor Smith."

"Say I can and I will."

"I can and I will."

"Are you married?"

"Yes."

"How long?"

I hesitated. None of his damn business, I thought. "109 years."

"Hahaha!" he barked. "I was married that long too, but I am in the middle of a divorce."

"Hmmm."

"Now I have a fox in my bed."

Silence.

"In fact, my goal is to see all long-term marriages end." Richard smiled.

"Oh."

He stood up. I stood up. He opened the door for me.

"Off you go," he said.

I walked to my car parked at the east side of Walgreen's off Central Avenue. What was I getting into? Again.

I dodged bikers on the sidewalk, staggering intoxicated homeless, and pushy panhandlers. Colorful Route 66. I liked it.

So Richard had a fox in his bed?

Once upon a time I slept with a lynx.

Christina Squire

Chapter 8

I had a lot to do before the fall semester started! I registered for 12 hours of graduate classes: Introduction to Graduate Studies, Children's Theatre, Acting on the Modern Stage, and African Dance. Well! I needed the exercise! I got all the paperwork for Professor Smith to transfer the graduate hours in English I took non-degree to my Master's Program. I walked all the way to the Physical Plant and got keys to Theatre X and to the Theatre Office.

I met with Professor Block, "Sam, please", to discuss my assistantship responsibilities. He looked as young as my son Peter! But he was very nice and earnest. 150 people had registered for Theatre Appreciation. I reserved books and movies at the Fine Arts Library. I copied the syllabus, the contact sheets, and the reading requirements. Here I was in my forties standing at a xerox machine like I did in my teens and twenties as a student employee. Talk about circular time.

Clarence often swished by me in the copy room to use the fax machine and smirked. But he always helped when the machine jammed and entertained me with snarky comments about the faculty. He said Richard

Smith brow-beat the rest of the faculty, because even though he was a full professor in the Department of Cinematic Arts, Richard overruled the Chair by scheduling the plays he wanted in Theatre X.

I wondered why Louise Snider, the Chair, always ignored me. A week before the semester began, she always whizzed by the copy room without a glance and walked by me in the hall without a greeting. I thought she was just busy and overwhelmed. When classes started in August I had to ask her a question about access to the Theatre X. I saw her scurrying down to the basement classrooms.

"Excuse me, Louise." I said catching up to her.

Nothing. She sped up.

"I need to ask you a question."

"What?" She kept moving with her back to me.

"I need access to Theatre X—"

She never turned around. "Get a key card from Clarence." She turned a corner.

She looked my age and had a wiry, tiny, tightly wound body. She taught acting and script analysis. Louise never acknowledged my presence. Nothing like feeling welcome in a department! Clarence said that was because Richard was my advisor. She did not approve of the Irish plays line-up. And I was part of it. "Don't take it personally, girlfriend!" he said. But I did.

Clarence had degrees in studio art and accounting. I wondered why he was where he was. Power. He ran the office like a SS queen.

I suddenly realized I did not even have time to think about my Inspector.

Chapter 9

I dropped off the tons of copied material to Sam and walked down the hall to Richard's office. He needed to approve my non-degree graduate hours. I passed a couple walking arm and arm. One woman was in her 50's, smoking an electronic cigarette, and holding tightly to an elderly woman. I smelled pineapple. I started to knock on Richard's door when I heard a raspy voice: "Are you involved with HIM?" I turned to the women. The older one walked up to me invading my personal space.

"He's my graduate advisor—" I said.

"Let me tell you something!"

"OK."

"Do you know what he did?" she asked.

"No," I said clutching my transcripts to my chest.

She pushed the vaping woman in front of me. She was short, pale, baggy-eyed with inky black hair in a blunt cut with long bangs. She wore beige, shapeless clothes. She looked depressed.

"He left my daughter, Marnie!"

I looked at Marnie. She sucked away looking bored. "I'm sorry," I said.

"After 38 years of marriage! Two children! Three grandchildren!" Mother ranted.

"I…"

"And all those Latin American plays he directed? She translated them all! And she was the dramaturge! My daughter! Ph.D. in Romance Languages! She's the brilliant one!" Mother yelled.

"I…"

Richard opened his door.

"You!" Mother screamed.

"Caro," Richard said. "Can we meet another time?"

Mother pulled her daughter past me into Richard's office in a cloud of fruity vapor. He closed the door.

Wow. Drama. Again.

Chapter 10

I found more drama at home. All I wanted to do was change into yoga pants, tissue tee, and Crocs, make a BLT with 5,000 Nacho Cheese Doritos and a Diet Coke, get on the couch with my dog and read a book until everyone came home from school and work.

I checked the front porch for mail. There was a large package from OnlineFabricStore. I was going to direct Beckett's *Act Without Words II* that was about two people who lived in sacks. I found a couple of used large burlap coffee bags on line. My actors will smell of coffee but too bad. Also I found a large manuscript with a big black bow tied around it. A note written in red ink was slipped under the ribbon:

"Hi Caro! My newest book! Please read and let me know what you think! Love, Tina."

Tina was one of my oldest friends and the most prolific writer. I had read two of her other manuscripts. She still had not found a publisher, but she continued to write. I admired her. She wrote potboilers, but people read those things. I was touched that she valued my feeble opinion. I felt like my life was a potboiler.

I made my lunch and sat down on the couch with the manuscript. I read:

AMUSE BOUCHE
(The Perfect Mouthful)

Chapter 1

Elena stepped out of her car. She took a huge breath of sea air from the Gulf of Mexico. Oh she was so scared!

(Oh no…another poor little thing. Harrumph.)

I couldn't take another poor distressed woman who eventually has more sex more often than anyone can imagine. No more women cooling their *como se llamas* in between wild and woolly encounters. I closed the manuscript. Sorry, Tina, but I was busy! I had all this work to do in Graduate School! I had to pay attention to my family! And I didn't need to fantasize about sex anymore! I knew what all the fuss was about! Maybe I will even write my own potboiler someday! I could not give Tina the attention she deserved. She needed to find a writing critique group. I'll recommend she contact Southwest Writers.

I slid the manuscript under the couch and flipped through the rest of the mail.

Something from Alphonse and Morrell Attorneys at Law. What? I ripped opened the envelope. I was being deposed next week! For the case of the state versus Olive Walters. Olive!!! Her! Why? I got a sudden headache in my eye! I had a flashback of her standing over me when I was in a hospital bed; reeking of gin and waving a sharp chopstick she'd pulled out of her bun. She confessed for crying out loud! Will this ever end?

I was ready to jump out of my skin. Olive had gotten to me again! I had to move. I tossed the coffee sacks in my car and drove back to the university.

I walked by the open door of the Theatre Office with the sacks draped over my arms. Louise was standing next to Clarence's desk.

"Where are you going, girlfriend?" Clarence called out.

I stopped. "Storing sacks for the Beckett play I am going to direct."

Louise gave me a stony glance. Thank you for asking me about the play, Louise. You are so supportive of my studies, I thought maliciously.

"What are you going to put in there? Bodies?" he asked.

"Actually, yes," I said.

"Creepy Beckett," Clarence said.

"Live ones, boyfriend," I said.

"That's no fun."

There was a class going on in Theatre X. I walked behind the thick black curtains to the prop room where I stored the bags. I ripped a page out of my Minion small notebook, wrote my name on it, and fastened it to the bags with a paper clip I found on the floor. I should have added Do Not Touch! People! I was ready for rehearsals to start in a few weeks. I was on top of things. Except for Olive, my mind was clear.

Christina Squire

Was my Inspector deposed, too?
My brain fled. My heart raced.

Chapter 11

I collapsed on a hallway bench after the deposition. I was exhausted. The lawyers for the defense and prosecution were very professional. But direct and to the point. Under oath I swore that I saw the ruby under the handicapped lift. No, I was not aware that Olive had lost a ruby out of her ring. Yes, I had met her before at Mariposa Gallery. Yes, I noticed then that she had a skull ring with ruby eyes. No, a ruby was not missing in her ring. No, Inspector Hutchinson did not know her at that time. Yes, I introduced them that night after we found the ruby. Yes, the lift rose up because I accidently hit the switch with my shoulder. Yes, I was in the handicapped closet with Inspector Hutchinson. No, I had not discussed looking for a ruby with the Inspector before we went in. Yes, he suggested going into the handicapped closet. Yes, it was a private place in the midst of a crowded museum. Yes, we wanted a private place. Yes, to get close. God I felt like I was exposed as a wanton woman. Well…

I sat there breathing deeply in pantyhose, ugly black old lady stacked shoes, black knee-length skirt, an

Christina Squire

industrial uplift bra and lilac polyester blouse buttoned up to my chin. No eye-liner. Soft combed short hair. No Bedhead Manipulator finger spiked do! Diamond studs in my ears, pearls roped around my neck and a delicate sapphire bracelet completed the staid persona I was hoping to project. I never wore those clothes but hauled them out to look demure. And earnest. And modest. So much for costuming. The truth was out. But why was I deposed? There must be an issue with the damn ruby.

My head finally stopped spinning. I walked to the elevator. The door opened. There was my Inspector. He wore a gray linen suit, blue gingham shirt and a navy tie. My knees weakened. I put one hand on the wall to keep from falling. James stepped out, put his hands around my waist, pulled me into the elevator, and hit the ground floor button. We went down. His hands stayed on my waist. I wrapped my arms around his waist. We stared at each other. We smiled. The elevator clunked to a stop. The door opened. He took my hand. We walked out of the courthouse and down four blocks to the Hotel Andaluz.

Chapter 12

"What's this?" James finally spoke when his hand moved under my skirt as we were locked in a passionate embrace.

"Support hose," I sighed.

We burst out laughing.

I flung an arm and leg over James. My heart finally started to beat normally after quite an explosive reunion. He held me tightly in his arms.

"James," I said.

"Mrs. Steele."

"Mrs. Steele?" I shrieked. "Seriously?" I rolled over on my back, laughing.

James moved down my body. "You will always be Mrs. Steele to me."

I stretched up both arms and grabbed the top of the headboard. "As you wish, Inspector Hutchinson."

James ordered room service from the hotel's Mas Tapas and Vino Restaurant. We sat at the room's small round table and wolfed down grilled artichokes, hot gouda with chorizo, *gambas fritas*, and Dos Equis beer.

"Were you ever going to tell me you were in town?" I asked.

"Yes. I knew you were busy starting the Fall semester in graduate school and—"

"What?"

"And that your deposition was at nine today."

"How did you know?"

"Max told me. I ran into him last week at the Flying Star on Rio Grande. We had lunch."

"On a school day he was twenty miles away from Highland High School! What in the hell was he doing down there?"

"Language, Mrs. Steele. Max said his Biology class was on a field trip to the Nature Center. You forgot to pack him a sack lunch."

"Oh that boy! Field trip my ass... What were you doing in the North Valley, James?"

"Looking."

"Looking for what?"

James stood up. "Come here, Mrs. Steele."

"No! Tell me what you were looking for!"

Somehow I ended up out of my chair and back on the bed. "You better tell me!" James was at task. "Don't distract me!" I was laughing and crawling away from him. He kept pulling me back.

"Wait," he said.

"No! Now!" Then I reconsidered. "Ok...later." I forgot all about the North Valley.

We lay face to face on our sides for a long time. I was so content and calm. I felt safe. I twisted his

34

beautiful dark auburn hair around my fingers. He was slowly moving his hand up and down the back of my legs. Every so often he leaned over to gently kiss the scar in my side where I had been stabbed months ago after discovering the museum forgeries.

"So you were deposed, too," I said.

"Yes."

"Why us?"

"I heard Olive insisted that she confessed under the influence of opioid pain killers she was on for her broken wrist. She claimed someone planted the ruby in the handicapped lift to incriminate her. She was framed. She blamed me. She blamed you."

"She's crazy."

"Like a fox."

"That reminds me!" I pushed James over, pounced on top and straddled him.

"Oof," he said. I was a sturdy woman.

I pressed my hands on his chest. "My graduate advisor told me that he divorced his wife and now has a fox in his bed."

"Does he now," James gasped.

"Yes he does now, and I thought you were a—" James suddenly held my hand up to his face. He bit my inner wrist.

"I was right," I said.

I sucked on my bitten wrist and looked at James. No blood. Then I bent down and put my teeth on his neck. He froze. I got a strange thrill feeling his strong, warm pulse against my lips. My heart was beating at the same time. Then I ran the tip of my tongue over his jaw and into his mouth where his tongue softly met mine.

***

I struggled back into my deposed clothes. It was after five. I had nothing planned for dinner. My mind crazily jumped from total ecstasy to buying a Sprouts Happy Roasted Chicken. James took me in his arms.

"So good-bye?" I whispered.

"I'm here to stay, Mrs. Steele."

"What?"

"The Albuquerque Police Department hired me... and I was looking for a place to live." I stared at him. "I'll walk you to your car."

Chapter 13

I put the roasted chicken and carton of deli potato salad on the counter. Max, John and Douglas were staring at me. I washed my hands. I needed to wash a lot more than my hands.

Max stood next to me. "Chicken again? Why are you dressed like that?"

I ignored him and took fresh greens out of the refrigerator to make a salad.

"You know I don't like potato salad, Mom!" Douglas said.

"Zap some Stouffer's mac and cheese," I said as I threw lettuce in a bowl.

"Where have you been?" John asked.

"I was deposed, remember? Then my sacks arrived. I had to store them in the Theatre X prop room. What a mess that was!"

"Come outside and have a glass of wine. I want to hear about it."

"Mom has beer breath," Max said.

I glared at Max. "If it's any of your business, which it's not, I joined a gathering in the graduate lounge after

I straightened out the prop room. And I know about Flying Star!" I realized immediately that I exposed myself.

"Then you know Inspector Hutchinson is moving here," Max said.

"Really? I learn something new every day," I said. I had to make an exit.

"What about that Inspector moving here?" John turned to Max.

"Albuquerque Police Department hired him. He didn't tell you, Mom?"

"I ran into him on his way to give a deposition, and he briefly mentioned he saw you. That's all."

"That's all?" John asked.

"I must bathe," I said.

I left them standing in the middle of the kitchen.

I sank into the water and sucked on my wrist. All the sucking, licking and biting going on today. So not me. But I liked it a lot. I liked it all a lot. I could not get enough of him. What was I going to do with James living here? He might take up all my time. I'd have to drop out of school.

Idiot.

I did not like becoming a world class liar. But maybe I could use this skill to my advantage. How did the routine go:

"I can't act."

"Have you ever told a lie?"

"Yes."

"Then you can act."

Small comfort for a liar.

Chapter 14

I spent the next day assisting Sam in his Theatre Appreciation class, sat around a conference table in Introduction to Graduate Studies to discuss *Hedda Gabler*, studied the Beckett play I was going to direct while I ate my sack lunch, and then went to African Dance. My body moved joyfully to the loud, wild beat of ten manly shirtless drummers. I tried to follow my beautiful teacher who was from Uganda. I felt alive. All over again.

Thank goodness for art, because I did not know what will happen with James. I had no illusions. But he should have texted me today.

I was walking out of Carlisle Gym when the dancer from Mexico came down the hall, clicking on her Flamenco shoes, flanked by two husky men with guitars slung over their shoulders. She glanced at me and stopped.

"I saw you outside of Richard's office. I want to warn you. He is a...how you say?" she tried to find the right word in English.

"Predator," one of the guitarists said.

"That's terrible," I said.

"Something has to be done about him. He can't act like that! I've told my graduate advisor about him. She told me that I am not the only one who has complained."

"My name is Caro. I just started the graduate program in theatre. Thank you for warning me."

"Nice to meet you, Caro. I'm Isabel. I am getting an MFA in Dance." We shook hands. "These are my friends Vincente and Joaquin." The men nodded. "They accompany the flamenco classes."

"Good to meet you all," I said.

"Remember he is the devil," Isabella whispered. "Watch yourself!"

"I'll keep that in mind, Isabel."

I went into the Theatre Office to check my mailbox. Clarence was getting ready to go home.

"You look all dewy. Afternoon delight?" he snarked.

"Not today, Clarence. African Dance."

"Sure. Whatever you say." He sprayed his desk with Lysol and wiped it off with a paper towel.

"I got an earful about Professor Smith from a dance grad student—" I said.

"The old goat," Clarence sneered.

"She was very upset!"

"Yeah…the head of Dance was in here talking to the Chair. I heard her shouting through the closed door. Richard is intimidating her dancers. I heard her say that he upset one of her students so badly that she had a seizure in his office."

"Horrible! What can be done?"

"Girlfriend! Hello! This is the university! Richard

has tenure in the Cinematic Arts Department. He's a full professor. He's published. Answer? Not one thing unless he's caught buggering the bursar."

"I heard that in a movie somewhere."

"*Educating Rita.* Life imitates art, Caro."

"Don't I know it."

"I'm off to the gym. Have to keep my girlish figure."

Christina Squire

Chapter 15

I went downstairs. I had an acting class at 6:00. We were doing scenes from Ionesco's *The Bald Soprano*. I was playing Mary, the maid. So much fun! I loved Theatre of the Absurd. Made sense of life to me in a mystifying way. I liked surprise. I liked mystery. Life was absurd most of the time. These plays made me want to stop taking myself so seriously. I had a long way to go, however.

My inner critic was interrupted by a piercing scream coming from Theatre X. Then "Oh my God!" and "Call the police" and "I'm going to throw up." I started running toward the black box. Classes emptied. Students ran through opened doors.

"Stay out!" Robert Hale, the set design teacher, barred the way in.

"What happened?" Everyone yelled.

"You don't want to see it," Robert said.

Louise, the chair, pushed by all of us and brushed Robert aside. She came back out immediately talking

43

on her cell phone, rapidly walking away. I heard her say "sack" and "Richard" and "head". Being no stranger to murder, I ran after her. I had to know! "Please tell me what happened," I said to her back.

Louise stopped. She turned around. "Our distinguished professor finally lost his head."

Chapter 16

A woman came screaming down the hall. She was waving her cell phone. She stopped in front of Louise and grabbed her shoulders. "I got a text! Where is he?" she cried.

Louise just stared at the twisted face in front of her. The 40-something year old woman had long red hair (too red!), wore a green camisole revealing a very generous milky white cleavage, skin-tight jeans and five-inch heels. Was she the fox?

"Tell me!" she howled. "I have to see him!"

"Brianne Morgan get your hands off me," Louise said. "You cannot see Richard's body." Brianne collapsed on the floor and sobbed. "Oh…And his head is missing."

Brianne fainted.

I felt like fainting but got over it when I saw Lt. Jane Keyes coming down the hallway with my Inspector! Oh! They stopped at Brianne's crumpled body.

"She just fainted," Louise said. James and Jane stepped over her.

"Mrs. Steele," James said as he passed by.

Jane nodded in my general direction.

45

Oh!

Well, weren't they a cozy pair. Jane Keyes of the UNM Police Department did help a little solving the murder at the Art Museum. But what was my Inspector doing at UNM again? Why wasn't he out in the city busting meth labs and gang bangers?

Several people followed them in Hazmat suits and rolling a gurney.

Louise left. I wasn't going anywhere! I looked at Brianne. A nice face. Out cold. I took a small dance concert poster off a bulletin board. I sat down next to her. I patted her hand. I fanned her with the poster. She started groaning. Her eyelids fluttered. "Is it true?" she murmured.

"Yes," I said.

"What am I going to do?" She squeezed my hand.

"I don't know. I'm so sorry."

My Inspector and Lt. Keyes came out of Theatre X and walked towards us.

"Was that your coffee sack in the prop room?" James asked.

Chapter 17

"What are you doing here?" I asked still holding Brianne's hand.

"Do you know him?" Brianne asked.

"A little bit."

"Inspector Hutchinson has been assigned to this case, Caro," Lt. Keyes said. "I asked for him. He knows the university, and we work well together."

"Do you now?" I stood up. Brianne sat up. James looked like he was trying not to smile. But not succeeding. That made me mad!

"Mrs. Steele, I repeat," James said. "Was that your sack in the Theatre X prop room?"

"I want a lawyer," I said.

"Don't be so dramatic, Caro!" Lt. Keyes said. "We're not accusing you of anything. We need to establish a time line when the sack was in there. Your name was pinned on it."

"Then why did you ask?"

James took a deep breath and took out a notebook.

"When did you put it in the prop room?"

"Let me check my calendar, Inspector." I whipped out my cell phone. "Let's see, it was the day before the deposition." I made a big business of looking intently at my phone. Scrolling leisurely up with my fingertip.

"OK, three days ago," James said quickly and scribbled something. Jane gave him a surprised look.

"Why, you are so right! How did you know? And actually I put two sacks in there." I was furious with him. He never contacted me after our afternoon together and spoke to me now like I was some stranger off the street.

James narrowed his beautiful green eyes. I blinked my stubby eyelashes at him. God help me if didn't I bite my tongue to keep a straight face. "I'm going to ask around to see if anyone saw anything," he said and walked toward the noisy crowd of students gathered far down the hallway. They stopped talking and looked wide-eyed at him. He looked so good, I thought. I was hopeless.

Jane was staring at me. What was her problem?

Brianne's wails interrupted my agitated thoughts. The forensic team came out of Theatre X followed by more Hazmat suited people pushing a dolly with a covered thin, long lump on top of it.

"Who did this to Richard?" she cried.

"We'll find out," Jane said. "And we'll need to contact you for questioning. Please give us your number."

"I'm going to throw up," Brianne said, stood up and wobbled out on her heels.

Jane turned to me. "I need to talk to you alone."

Chapter 18

"Let's go outside on the loading dock," I said. My heart was pounding. I felt a weird vibe from her.

We walked up the stairs and out the huge metal doors. I saw a tow truck hauling a car out of the loading zone. When will students learn? I sat down on the concrete steps. Jane stood over me. "Well?" I asked.

Jane sat down. "I heard you mention that you were deposed a few days ago. I was, too."

"Oh?"

"For the case of the state versus Olive Walters."

"And?"

"The lawyers questioned me at length about what I thought about your relationship with Inspector Hutchinson."

"Really?" I needed a cigarette. Badly.

"Yes."

"And?"

"I said at first I thought you both were close friends since you worked on the observatory murder together."

"At first?"

"Then I saw you dancing at the Art Museum opening and watched you both go down to the lower gallery."

49

"Hmmm." I was getting light-headed knowing where this was heading. I could not blow this off as none of her damn business, because now clever Olive had made it Jane's business. So I will be cool and calm. Acting.

"I arrived for my deposition and watched as James swept you into the elevator."

"Hmmm."

"So I told the lawyers what I witnessed. And now I'm telling you."

"All right."

Jane stood up. So did I. Her slender, crisply tailored six foot tall body towered over my well-fed, Target dressed 5'8" one, but I stood straight and assumed an air of vitality. Acting. Again. She started to walk away but stopped. "James was accused of planting evidence in New Orleans. He was cleared but after a long, humiliating investigation."

"Oh?"

"He never told you?"

Silence.

"If I were you…" Jane said. Well, you're not, I wanted to snark, but I didn't. My mouth was too dry. "If I were you," she repeated, "I would stay away from him. Olive's lawyers are building a case against you, I believe. They will be looking for more evidence to prove that you both planted that ruby in the handicapped lift."

I swallowed air then opened my big mouth. "They'll need a lot more evidence than a dance and an elevator encounter."

"They'll find it, Caro."

Chapter 19

James appeared. "I wondered where you both were."

Silence.

"What's wrong?" he said.

Silence.

"Are you done here?" Lt. Keyes asked him.

"I didn't get much from the students. We'll interview faculty and staff tomorrow. And we have to get a head."

"Right." She turned toward the doors to the main building. She looked behind her. "Are you coming?"

"I'll meet you back at the station. I want to talk to Mrs. Steele."

Lt. Keyes bit her lip and shook her head. "Will you walk?"

"I'll give him a lift," I said.

"Right." She left.

My Inspector faced me. "What's wrong?"

"I am very upset! My graduate advisor's headless body was found in a sack for my Beckett play! His head is probably in my other sack!"

"Sounds very Beckett to me…"

"It does actually." I paused. Then rallied. "Jane

51

Keyes told me that you were investigated for planting evidence in New Orleans—"

"I was cleared."

"She told me. Good. But Olive's lawyers have probably pounced on that charge. And they have a strong suspicion that we are intimately involved—"

"We are, thank God."

He reached for me. I pushed him away. My eyes filled with tears. "And Jane was deposed and questioned if she witnessed any signs that we were having an affair—"

"She didn't tell me she was deposed."

"Well, she was. And she, when asked under oath, told them that she saw several moments of affection between us."

"Really now."

"Yes, James! Really! And she warned me that the lawyers are making a case against us for planting the ruby in the handicapped lift."

"That will never happen."

"And she recommended that I stay away from you."

"That will never happen."

"Oh no? Are you so sure of yourself? You never told me you were in town! And why! You never told me about New Orleans! I never heard from you after… after… I don't know what to think about you! It's like I've gone crazy! I've become a liar!" James moved closer. I pushed him away again. "I mean, you still call me Mrs. Steele! Does that help you create a distance from me: Temporary, transitory, ephem—"

Murder at Theatre X

James grabbed my upper arms. My hands pressed against his chest. "I don't want distance between us! Why do you think I moved here?" He kissed me hard.

I lost track of where I was for a while. Then I whispered, "I don't know what's going to happen to us."

"Let's not try to know."

I pulled his tie until we were nose to nose. "That's a line out of *The Bald Soprano*."

"I know."

"I love Ionesco."

"I love him, too."

Christina Squire

Chapter 20

We walked east on Central to my car parked next to Walgreen's. It was dark, but the street lights and stream of traffic lit up the sidewalk, the homeless, and bus stops with colorful people. We did not talk. I think we were both tired.

But I wasn't that tired.

"How is your wife?" I asked.

"Monique is in a sleep therapy sanitorium in Switzerland."

"So she graduated from the New Orleans clinic?"

"Yes. She's asleep in a beautiful place. For a longer time."

"Oh James! I'm sorry."

"Don't be. She is happier this way. She's peaceful. Life is too intense for her." James suddenly stopped. He looked at me. He was going to kiss me again. I hoped Olive's lawyers weren't trolling Central. But he said, "I'm starving."

"I know a pizza place."

I led him off Central to Carraro's on Vassar. We sat side by side at a corner table. We took out our phones.

I read texts from John wondering where I was. I replied that there was a murder at Theatre X. I was going to be held up for questioning. He texted back 'OMG' right away. Then: 'Is that Inspector there?' I tossed the phone back in my purse.

I read the menu. "What kind of pizza do you like, James?"

"Anything, Mrs. Steele."

We ordered a sausage and mushroom pie and beer.

"How are your boys?" James asked.

"Fine, fine, fine…. How is Claire?"

"Doing well at Colorado College. But I never imagined my daughter majoring in Chemistry. The only D I made in high school was in Chemistry."

"The only D I made in college was in Chemistry."

The waiter set two tall glasses of La Cumbre Elevated in front of us.

We clinked. "To chemistry," he said.

I drank and felt a warm chemical reaction bubbling throughout my body. Must be the beer or his knee touching mine.

We sat quietly. I picked up the unlit candle in the middle of the table. I put it down. I rummaged around in my purse for matches. I lit the candle. I pushed the salt, pepper, red pepper flakes, and Parmesan cheese to one side. I felt like there was so much to say but neither one of us said anything. Like my marriage. No chatting. Sometimes that was best. In the short term.

But I could not help myself.

"Well? Did you find a place in the North Valley?" I asked.

Murder at Theatre X

"Yes…a townhouse in Cimino Compound."

"Off Rio Grande Boulevard! Beautiful place. I knew someone who lived there. All adobe, vigas, brick floors…"

"Very New Mexico. Like the Abiquiu Inn casita."

I had an erotic flashback: Our bodies moving together. The fragrant pinon wood burning in the kiva fireplace…Flickering light over our skin. I wanted to crawl in his lap but our pizza came.

We devoured most of it and ordered another beer.

"So…do you want to know what I know about the dearly departed Professor Smith?" I asked.

"I always want to know what you know, but you can tell me tomorrow. I want to enjoy the remains of the day," James said. He took my hand. "I must tell you—"

"Are you going to eat the rest of that pizza?" Max! He pulled up a chair and plopped down.

I dropped James's hand.

Max smiled. James grinned.

"What are you doing here?" I yelled.

"Mom! Lower your voice! I'm playing pool in the back room! I told you that the church youth group was going out for pizza tonight!"

"At a bar? Where are your chaperones?"

"At the bar."

"Oh!" I got up. I saw Mr. and Mrs. Blake sitting on tall stools drinking martinis.

"What a progressive church," James said.

"It's a very holy place," Max said. "You should come to St. Luke's."

"I may do that."

57

I glared at Max as he ate the rest of our pizza. He was oblivious. "We have to go now. There's been a murder at the Theatre Department—"

"Mom! That university is a dangerous place!"

"—and Inspector Hutchinson has to get back and investigate."

Max stood up, wiped his hands and face on my napkin, and shook hands with James. "Good luck on this case, Inspector." Max gave me a hug. "See you at home, Mom."

James laughed and laughed as we walked two blocks to my car. "Max is a clever lad." He wiped his eyes on his sleeve.

"Isn't he, though. He could work for Olive's lawyers," I grumped.

Chapter 21

I dropped James off at the University Police Station. We had as much of a passionate good-bye as we could manage in the front seat of a VW Beetle in a parking lot with screamingly bright lights and a gearshift knob between us.

The only one to greet me when I came home was Suki. I put her outside. I saw a note from John on the kitchen table: 'Gone to see Douglas play. Hope you are OK.' I felt horrible! I forgot about the UNM Jazz Band's concert in Woodward Hall tonight. I forgot about a lot of things lately.

But I could not forget about the murder of Richard Smith! I needed to help my Inspector. I knew things!

I let Suki inside and ran a bath. I leaned back in the tub and thought about my Inspector. I wondered if he felt guilt. He did not have to go home every day and lie. His wife was a million miles away. I either had to make peace with the fact that I was an adulterer or leave John. Or never be with James again and return to being the good wife. I could not do that now. I could not. I could not think about this anymore, either. Instead my thoughts turned to all the helpful information about

Professor Smith that I will share with James...and that I had to order two more coffee bags.

I crawled into bed with Suki and read some performance theory handouts (major yawn).

Max came home. He sat at the foot of the bed. Suki rolled over on her back so he could scratch her tummy. He kept smiling at me. Or was he smirking? Or was he stoned? I decided to go on the attack. For once.

"Why didn't you go to your brother's concert?"

"I had a spiritual commitment. Why didn't you?"

"I had a professor's head in my coffee bag."

"You win, Mom!" He gave me a high five.

We burst out laughing so loudly that Suki gave us a gimlet eye and jumped off the bed.

Douglas walked in. "What's so funny?"

I got out of bed and hugged him. "Oh something silly. Sorry I missed your concert. There was a murder in Theatre X!"

"That's horrible, Mom! Who?" Douglas said.

"Professor Smith."

"Was that Inspector there?"

"Yes...So how was your performance, honey? I'm glad Dad could see you."

"We played well. Dad left at intermission. He's not home yet?"

"No, he isn't."

Chapter 22

I was asleep when John came home. The next morning I woke up just as he was leaving for work. I stomped up to him at the door. He stepped back. I was resplendent with bed head, wearing men's plaid boxer shorts and navy stretched out men's tank top.

"So you were at Douglas's concert?" I asked.

"Yes. So you were at a murder scene? You did not answer all my texts."

"I was in shock, John. Professor Smith's decapitated body was found in the Theatre X prop room in one of my sacks for the Beckett play. His head and my other sack are missing!"

"That's too bad, Caro." John opened the door.

"I have some leads Inspector Hutchinson can look into—"

"So he was there. I'm sure you both will have success. As usual." He walked out on the porch.

"Douglas said you left at intermission," I said to his back.

John turned around. "I had to pick up my partner Steve at the airport."

"That took half the night?"

61

"We had a beer and discussed the client he audited. Business. OK?"

"Discussing auditing over beer? What fun." I smiled.

"Discussing murder over beer? What fun." John smiled, lightly kissed me and went out the screen door.

Well! Weren't we the Lunts of Albuquerque? We could out perform that famous acting couple any day of the week!

Max! He must have sung like a canary.

Louise cancelled all classes the next day. She held a department meeting in the Art History lecture hall. Clarence sent out a mass e-mail calling for mandatory attendance for faculty, staff, and students. The fox must have gotten word. Was Brianne a student? She was sitting in the front row dressed in black: plunging V-necked black mini dress, black hose, black high heels. Her long bright red hair was tied back with a fat black ribbon. Her snow-white cleavage heaved with every sniff she took into a black lace handkerchief. Louise was sitting on the raised platform with my Inspector and Lt. Keyes. She kept staring at Brianne. James and Jane glanced at her often, also. Well, who wouldn't?

My Inspector stepped up to the lectern. One again I found myself listening to him talk about the murder of a professor. I remembered being in the lounge at Physics and Astronomy with the staff while he questioned us about the death of one of their professors. So

Murder at Theatre X

much has happened since then. Seemed so long ago. Was I older and wiser? Well, older. Circular time? My priorities were so different now. Was that a good thing? At least I was not a suspect. I hoped.

James had his and Lt. Keyes' contact information on the board. Anyone should not hesitate to call them about any information they may have about the murder no matter how insignificant. Professor Smith was decapitated, and his head still had not been found. Authorities were still searching the Fine Arts Building, the Carlisle Gym Dance space, and the Cinematic Arts offices and classrooms in the five story humanities building. Police were combing the grounds around the Fine Arts Center, trash bins, and parking structure. His home was thoroughly searched.

I was sitting next to Clarence. He leaned over and whispered: "I know you and your tasty Inspector will put your *heads* together and find Professor Smith's heavy head—"

"You're real funny, Clarence. And he's not my Inspector."

"Then can I have him?"

Christina Squire

Chapter 23

"Any questions?" Lt. Keyes asked.

Silence.

Louise stood up. "Services are pending until notification of his family. The department will send out an e-mail. I want you all to cooperate with Inspector Hutchinson and Lt. Keyes. Counseling will be available. Professor Smith's classes will be cancelled. I will allow those enrolled in them to register for another class for credit even though the deadline has past. I made special arrangements with the Dean of Students. I have the waivers in my office. Thank you."

"Anything else?" James asked.

Silence.

"Then Lt. Keyes and I need to question some of you privately. The Chair has provided us with contact information."

The crowd started buzzing as they left the auditorium. I walked toward the door with Clarence.

"Mrs. Steele," I heard James say. I turned. "Can you come with us, please?"

My stomach flipped over.

"Go, girl!" Clarence hissed in my ear. "And ditch the Amazon."

Jane, James and I sat in a private room in the Fine Arts Library down the hall.

"Ok, Mrs. Steele. Please tell us what you know about Richard Smith," James said.

"He was my graduate advisor," I said.

"We already know that," Jane said.

"Of course you do! The campus police are on top of things, as usual," I said.

"Drop the attitude, Caro. We're all working for the same—"

"Please just tell us what you know, Mrs. Steele," James said. All business.

I could be all business, too. With the best of them.

I started out with the time I overheard screaming coming from his office. I told them that the screamer's name was Isabel, no I did not know her last name, and that she was an MFA student in Dance. I mentioned that she saw me a few days later after my dance class surrounded by flamenco guitarists Vincente and Joaquin. No I did not know their last names. Isabel told me that Professor Smith was a predator and called him a devil in Spanish.

James and Lt. Keyes took notes.

"And he gave me the creeps. He asked about the films I had been in. He wanted to know if I ever had a romantic role. I said no. He was surprised. Said I was pretty…and that there where were parts out there for me where I could make a lot of money…As if! I couldn't even get an extra part in *Breaking Bad* last year. Big jerk."

Jane shook her head as she wrote something down. James tossed his pen down on the table, leaned back in his chair and crossed his arms. Jane glanced at him.

Then I told them about seeing the Professor's wife, who he was divorcing, and her mother in the hallway on the way to his office. No, I do not know their names, either. The mother was very angry with Richard and yelled horrible things about him to me.

"What things?" Jane asked.

"That her daughter was the talented one, and he was a piece of shit to leave her after 38 years of marriage."

"What did the wife say?" James asked. He started writing again.

"Nothing. She was sullenly vaping…Then Clarence told me that Louise Snider, the Chair, was very angry with Professor Smith for scheduling all the Irish Plays in Theatre X without consulting her. Clarence said that he bossed everyone around in the department because he was a Cinematic Arts professor.

"What was he doing in Theatre and Dance?" Jane asked.

"Clarence said he had a joint appointment."

"Clarence knows a lot," James said and turned to the Lieutenant. "We have to question him."

"Oh," I added. "And the professor had a fox in his bed."

"What?" Jane exclaimed. James bent his head like he was writing notes but not before I saw him biting his lip.

"Yes…the learned Professor Smith told me that he

had a fox in his bed. I bet it was the woman who fainted in the hallway and was sitting in the front row today. I know you both noticed Brianne Morgan."

"Academics…," I heard Jane mutter.

"And Richard told me that his aim now was to see all long term marriages end," I said.

"What a prize," Jane said and looked at me. I flushed. Did she think my own long marriage was in trouble? Did I? I did! She knew I was attracted to James. I suddenly felt very uncomfortable. My feeling of pride knowing all this information about Professor Smith withered under her gaze.

"Did he ever talk about your program of studies?" Jane asked.

"Yes. Of course," I said. "Do you want to know what it is?"

"Not really."

James quickly wrapped up this Q & A. "Anything else, Mrs. Steele," James asked.

"Nothing I can think of right now," I murmured.

"You've been so helpful. Thank you for your time," he said.

"I'm here to help," I said.

Jane gave me another look. James seemed to find an imaginary spot on the ceiling.

Chapter 24

I took two flights of stairs down to the Loading Dock. I stood next to a dumpster and lit a cigarette. I watched a huge white truck pull up. Two men got out, opened the back, lowered a ramp, walked up into the back, and came out pushing large, blue recycling bins. They rolled them past me.

"Smoking will kill you," one guy said over his shoulder.

Everyone's a critic, I thought, but I put out my ciggie and stuck it through a crack in the dumpster lid. "Excuse me," I said to them. They stopped rolling. "How often do you collect recycling here?"

They tipped the bins upright. The robust one answered, "Twice a month. We did this building yesterday, but we are back today, because the new Dean had the Library get rid of old journals, magazines and manuscripts. Fire hazard, you know. And they're all on line, anyway."

"Of course," I said like I knew it all. But I did have an idea forming in my head. "Where is the College Fine Arts recycling from yesterday now?"

69

"At the UNM Recycling Center."

"Have they already been recycled?"

"Not yet. Bins are emptied into dumpsters. When those are filled up the city comes and hauls them away. Hey, we have to go. We have other buildings to do."

"Of course you do. And thank you for your time!" The men tipped the large bins back on their wheels and rolled into the Fine Arts Center.

I lit another cigarette. Just then my Inspector and Lieutenant Keyes came out on the Loading Dock. They didn't notice me lurking by the trash. They walked toward his black Jeep Commander parked in a reserved space. (I fondly remembered spending time with him in the roomy back seat. But enough of going down memory lane. I will not be distracted!) I tossed my Marlboro Light away and skipped after them. They were talking seriously. Well! I had something serious to say!

I stopped. No more wagging my tail behind me—eager to please—full of information. I will check out my theory. I may get a head. And my other sack! Probably at the same time.

Chapter 25

Since all classes were cancelled for the day, and I had pinto beans and green chili in the crockpot for dinner, I drove to the UNM Recycling Department. I wandered around the roads behind the Physical Plant on the North Campus. I finally recognized the white square trucks with the round green logo parked behind a tall chain-link fence. I stopped and got out of my car. A huge garage and smaller brown stucco building were way down at the other end of the lot that was filled with enormous topless dumpsters on wheels. They were draped in ragged, torn beige material that fluttered in the breeze. I saw a few seven foot squares of wire-wrapped crushed aluminum cans reflecting the sunlight. Smaller, lower, dumpsters were filled with cardboard and colored paper. It looked like a science fiction movie set. A dystopian, blighted, trashed out country. Eerie.

The gate was open. Could I walk in? Actually, I had to drive in or get ticketed by the johnny on the spot Campus Parking Services. A big sign said 'Official Vehicles Only'. Ok. I got in my car. I'll make an appointment, I thought, and come back later. I started the car. What was wrong with me? Why do I hesitate? What was I so afraid of? I drove into the lot.

No one rushed out to yell at me. I parked my car. I got out and walked to the garage. I saw a man sorting through a trough of twisted metal.

"Excuse me!" I said.

"Can I help you?" he asked.

"Yes! My name is Caroline Steele. I have some questions about recycling!"

"OK." The man took off his work gloves. He wore a stained, blue jumpsuit.

"Where is the recycling that was collected from the Fine Arts Center yesterday?"

"We just got paper from there. We've already separated the white from the colored and put them in separate dumpsters." He walked out to the big lot and gestured grandly. "Now all the white went into that 20 yarder over there." He pointed. This dumpster was high off the ground on big wheels. "Then we have the 12 yarders over here." He gestured. I noticed they sat level on the ground. "The colored paper goes in one and cardboard goes in the other."

"So you all have sorted everything that was collected yesterday."

"Yes, Ma'am."

Oh I hate being called ma'am! But he was so polite. Note to self to start coloring hair!

"And you just found paper?"

"Oh we always find some garbage. People! They think they can throw anything in a clearly labeled recycling only container! Go figure!"

"It's a shame…"

Murder at Theatre X

"Did you lose something, Miss?"

"Kinda sorta…So only university departments deliver their recycling here?"

"Now that is a real problem. We have people sneak in and put their recycling in our dumpsters! And they don't sort first! Then when the city comes and hauls a full one away to Master Fibers down on Edith, they complain that we don't sort! Gives us a bad name!"

"Sorry…Is there some way I can go through these?"

"You'll need a ladder to get up to the top of the 20 yarder. If you fell in, it would be like drowning in paper! I don't think you want to do that."

"But I want to."

"I'll have to talk to my supervisor."

"And I'll have to talk to my Inspector."

"What?"

"Nothing. Talking to myself. When will the city come to haul these away?"

"We call them when they're full. I'd say in a few days. Maybe a week."

"Thank you so much--" I read his badge. "—George!"

I drove out the Recycling Department's open gate and pulled to the side of the road. I texted my Inspector: 'Chat?'

Christina Squire

Chapter 26

"Yes," James pinged.

"Never mind," I typed.

He sent "?".

I threw the phone in my purse. I was so tired of everything and everyone. Tired of lying, tired of graduate school, tired of being married, tired of juggling, tired of cooking and all the household chores, tired of not trusting James, tired of my uncontrollable lust for him (not that tired), tired of doubt, tired of trying to please everyone, tired of being tired...My phone rang. And rang. James. I let it go to voice mail. I started the car and headed for home.

My phone rang again. James. Too bad. Let him squirm. (I could only hope he squirmed!) My phone exploded with pings of texts coming from him. Oh now he texts me! After I let him do wonderful things to my body all one afternoon, not a word! But I pulled over into the Campus Observatory parking lot. Ah... such memories. Poor departed Professor Cummings. Sad. Almost as sad as poor departed Professor Smith.

I finally took out my phone. "Movie? Need break." I read.

"?" I texted.

"2nite. *Cafe Society*. Downtown. 5:30."

"love Woody Allen"

"love him 2"

I thought about this for a nanosecond. I sent "CU".

I got to Central, turned right, and turned left on Second Street. I drove into the parking complex just past Gold. What was I doing? Walking into Century 14 Theatre, that's what, and seeing my Inspector waiting in the lobby.

He put his arms around me. "I should be at home," I whispered into his warm neck.

"Thank you for being here with me," he said.

People in the lobby were staring at us. We broke apart.

"Hungry?" he asked.

"Yes."

James bought two hot dogs, a small box of popcorn, and Cokes. We slathered our buns with mustard and relish.

We walked into an empty theatre.

"So where do you want to sit?" he asked, laughing.

"Gee, I can't decide!"

We chose the back row. The previews hadn't even started yet. Short bits promoting TV programs blasted from the screen. We devoured our hot dogs. Previews started. After each one, we'd comment "I don't think so", "maybe", "can't wait". A few more people came in and sat down front.

The movie began. He flipped up the armrest between us. He put his arm around me. He kissed me. I kissed him back. I put my head on his shoulder.

"I feel like a teenager," I said.

76

Murder at Theatre X

"Do you now?" James moved the box of popcorn out of the way.

He kissed me passionately. I grabbed his beautiful hair and kissed him back passionately.

I guess the movie was good.

Christina Squire

Chapter 27

"What did you want to chat with me about?" he asked as we rode the elevator up to the top of the parking structure. We did not take the stairs. My legs were too weak. I'd had a few moments with James during the movie. What movie?

"I saw something. Probably nothing. I'm not thinking clearly."

"I think you are."

The elevator door opened. I saw his Jeep Commander gleaming in the moonlight. I wanted to crawl in the back seat with him, but I walked slowly to my silver VW Beetle dreading the scene when I got home late.

I took out my keys and opened my car door then slammed it shut.

"What's wrong?" James asked.

I turned around. "I am sick and tired of living a double life! I have never done this before! I'm afraid—"

"Don't be afraid, Mrs. Steele."

We stared at each other.

"I think Professor Smith's head is in a recycling dumpster!" I blurted out.

He stepped back. "I beg your pardon?"

"James! His head may be in a dumpster at the University Recycling Department!"

"Why do you say that?"

"I spoke to some guys who were picking up recycling at the Fine Arts Center. They were pushing big bins on rollers. Made me suspicious! Then I went to the Recycling Department, and now I have a new best friend George who works there and told me more about recycling than I could imagine. And he said that people not affiliated with the university dump recycling in their bins! A problem he has!"

"Why would anyone put his head there?"

"Because it's mashed into pulp at Albuquerque Master Fibers and sent to Mexico!"

"Mexico?"

"Oh! It doesn't matter, James! Just an idea I had! Forget it!" I opened my car door.

James pulled me close. "I can't forget anything about you, Mrs. Steele."

Over his shoulder I saw a slender woman with long platinum hair walk by wearing a trench coat and black patent leather stiletto heels. She was holding the arm of a short, bald older man in a suit. She stopped. She caught my eye. Her blood red lips broke into a smile. She leaned over and whispered in the man's ear. He glanced at me. Then he clicked opened the door to a black Lexus.

I turned James around. "Olive," I said.

"And her lawyer."

We watched them drive off.

"She looked better with her hair in a French Roll," I said.

James laughed. "With chopsticks?"

"Don't scare me!"

James stopped laughing. "I don't want you walking up and down Central to your car anymore. You got stabbed and could have died last year! Get a reserve parking space close to the Fine Arts Center."

"John has applied for one."

"Good. Olive will stop at nothing to get revenge on us for finding the ruby that incriminated her. Olive is free and determined – she's like a runaway freight train."

"Now I'm really scared! But I will miss burning 100 calories every—"

"I don't want to lose you."

"Oh James," I whispered. My breath caught at this change of tone: serious, genuine, sincere. I could not speak.

He finally broke the silence and smiled. "I'd be so bored, Mrs. Steele."

I gently kissed him. "Well, Inspector Hutchinson, then I say death to boredom."

Christina Squire

Chapter 28

The house was quiet. I let Suki outside. Max appeared out of nowhere.

"Where were you?" he asked.

"I went to a movie."

"Alone?"

"No. I was with Inspector Hutchinson." I walked past him into the kitchen. "Have you eaten?"

"Yes. The chili was good." He was looking at my lips. "Looks like you've had another allergic reaction to ka—"

"Don't," I said and went into the bedroom. "Where is everyone?"

"Dad said he had a meeting. Douglas is out with friends."

"Ok. Excuse me. I'm going to take a bath."

Max took my hand. "Mom! Please! You and Dad can't go on like this much longer!"

I kissed his hand. "I love you, Max."

"I love you, too, Mom."

***

I took a lobster bath, poured a glass of wine, sat on the backyard deck and lit a ciggie. I thought about James warning me strongly about Olive. I worried about him, too. She saw us together: Ammunition for her case that we plotted to frame her for murder. I heard John drive up. He rummaged around in the kitchen. I could not think about Olive now. But maybe I should.

John barged out the screen door with a glass of wine. "Where have you been?" he asked as he sat down and stretched out his long legs.

I took a deep breath. I looked at the stars through the boughs of the backyard trees. The moon cast shadows on our pots of colorful geraniums bordering the deck. "Where have YOU been?"

"Working."

"At what?"

"Making a living."

"Oh is that what it's called now?"

"I can't take acting in this this charade of a marriage any longer! No phone call! No text—"

"You didn't let me know—"

"Where were you, Caro?"

"At a movie with James."

John stood up and loomed over me. "You have been having an emotional affair with that inspector! I'm not stupid."

"Hmmm." I blew out a stream of smoke.

"Oh! So it's physical?" He yelled. He picked up a Target mesh lawn chair and threw it off the deck.

84

I stood up. "Yes."

"For how long?"

"Not long...off and on."

"Why am I not surprised? We haven't had sex in months! When I even touch you, you act like cockroaches are crawling all over you..."

Max rushed outside. "Dad! Stop yelling! What's going on?"

"Your mother is fucking that inspector!"

Max moved between John and me. At 16 he was as tall as his Dad. "Calm down, Dad."

"After all I've done for her! See how she betrays me!" He pushed Max out of the way. "Shame on you!" he screamed in my face.

"After all YOU'VE done for ME?" I screamed. "Shame on yourself!"

John grabbed my arm. Once again Max moved quickly between us. "Dad! That's enough. It's late. The neighbors! You can talk about this tomorrow. You both are too upset now to make sense!"

"I'm not saying jack shit to your mother. I'm leaving."

"Dad! It's better to face your problems than run away from them."

Why didn't I hear this years ago? Why did I distract myself with reading, torture jobs, and daydreaming instead of dealing with reality. I did not say what I felt. I swallowed anger. I was not honest with John or myself. Until now.

John charged past us into the house.

"Are you going to be with Alice?" I called sweetly to his back.

Christina Squire

The front door slammed.

"Alice the secretary?" Max exclaimed.

Chapter 29

I slept like the dead.

I woke up late. Douglas and Max had left for school. Suki was in bed with me. I buried my face in her soft brown fur. I kissed her snout. I rubbed her warm tummy. I stroked her ears. I didn't want to get up, but I did. I let her out. I made my own fucking coffee. I felt good. Finally the elephant was out from under the table. Now what?

I had to go to school, that's what. I had projects due! I had to assist Sam in Theatre Appreciation. He was giving a four-week essay exam. I'll have to grade 150 of them. Joy. I better find two actors to be in bags and a goad operator. And make a goad! On wheels, for crying out loud. Beckett! Such a unique playwright. The Irish Festival had to go on, I thought. Posters were hung all over campus.

I had to watch my back. Olive was free.

I choked down a bowl of Cheerios with strawberries and blueberries. My hands shook as I applied eyeliner. Maybe I wasn't feeling that good.

"Now I know you feel overwhelmed," Sam said as we walked away from the lecture hall. I lugged the bluebooks in my Virgin of Guadalupe bag. "Just check off the key points. I don't care about spelling or punctuation. Do you think you can have them done by next week?"

"I will. Can I keep them in your office until I leave today?"

"Sure. I'll grade a few with you so you can get an idea of what I'm looking for."

I collapsed in the chair next to Clarence's desk. He continued typing, of course. Louise's door was closed, of course. The student helper was sitting at the other desk looking in a compact mirror applying lipstick. I heard laughter coming from the copy room. I sighed. No response. I sighed again loudly and dramatically with a slight trill.

Clarence slowly swiveled away from his computer and faced me. How did he get the part in his hair so straight? "What's wrong with you, girlfriend?"

"Everything."

"Trouble in paradise? Did the Amazon drag off your Inspector?"

"Oh Clarence! I have 150 exams to grade, and I have to find two actors who don't mind being in coffee sacks."

"Well, I know something." Clarence started counting off information on his perfectly formed fingertips. "Coffee sack. Head. Took call from Recycling Department for Louise. Heard scream behind door—"

"Oh my God! Clarence! Did they find his head there?" Oh I was a good detector!

"*No se, Chica.*"

"I have to text my Inspector!"

"Wait a minute…Bill! Alan!" he screeched.

Two handsome undergraduates came out of the copy room. "You bellowed?" Bill giggled and salaamed to Clarence. "Your wish is our command."

"Yeah, right. Caro needs two actors to be in a Beckett play. Are you boy toys busy?"

Bill and Alan looked at me. "What play?" Alan asked.

"*Act Without Words II*," I said.

"We'd have no lines?"

"No…pantomime: brushing teeth, combing hair, putting on clothes, some whistling, chewing a carrot, praying."

"We can do that!" Bill said and Alan nodded his head.

"You'd be in big sacks in between the physical action."

"Brilliant!" They both said.

I got their cell phone numbers and e-mail addresses before they left.

"Thanks, Clarence," I said.

"Now text that fetching piece of flesh."

Christina Squire

Chapter 30

Text nothing! I was driving over there! My next class wasn't until the late afternoon. I race-walked to my car. When I turned off University onto Tucker I saw UNM Police and APD vehicles parked along the street. I parked illegally in the G lot and jumped out of my car. I walked past a Campus Police officer who was playing on his cell phone.

"You can't go over there, Ma'am," he said.

(Ma'am, my ass!) "I am Caroline Steele. I work with Inspector James Hutchinson of the Albuquerque Police Department."

He stared at me dressed in cropped black tights, Giant Steps concert tee, jean jacket and Sketcher Go-Walks.

"Plain clothes division," I said. He should have asked for my ID, but he was not one of the best and the brightest. "What's going on?"

"A head was found in a dumpster."

"I'm on it!" I walked quickly away. I had to stop myself from skipping with joy. Yes! I knew it!

The gate to the Recycling Department lot was closed and crisscrossed with crime tape. I saw my Inspector and Lt. Keyes in there talking to people. I hooked

91

my fingers through the chain link fence and shouted "James". Everyone looked at me. I saw my new best friend George. "Hi, George!" I yelled and waved. He waved back.

"You found it?" I called out to my Inspector and Jane. They both made their way slowly (too slowly!) towards me.

James answered when they (finally!) got to the gate. "Yes, Mrs. Steele. In the cardboard recycling dumpster."

"I was right!" Once again my detecting and observational powers resulted in a major break in a case. I felt strong and able.

"Good work, Caro. Thank you," Jane said.

"You're welcome, Jane," I said.

James wore those damn Ray Bans. I could not see his expression. "We still have a lot to do here, Mrs. Steele," he said.

"Of course," I said. "I just wanted to know!"

I trudged back to my car. James could have thanked me! Was he in full-blown police mode? All in charge in front of Lt. Keyes and the Recycling staff? I helped him a lot. He better thank me later.

Now who murdered the esteemed professor? I will give that some thought after I go to class, go home, make dinner, grade exams, and plot my divorce.

Chapter 31

Douglas, Max, Sally and I sat quietly around the kitchen table after eating the tacos I made for dinner. I had called my sister in tears when I got home. The events of the last 24 hours came crashing down on me. I was a crumpled heap. I could tell John had been by that day to get clothes, shoes and toiletries. His closet door and drawers were wide open. I get the picture, John, I thought maliciously.

Sally rushed over after her Yoga class. I was so glad she was with us. She was a steady, loyal presence in our lives. Although she did hiss at me when I let her in: "I hope you know what you're doing."

Sally finally broke the tense silence. "Here we are. Safe and sound. Warm and fed. We must be grateful."

Silence.

"Are you divorcing Dad?" Douglas asked me.

"I don't know. We are both so angry right now—"

"You're both unhappy. Maybe you need time apart, Mom," Max said.

"That makes sense, honey," Sally said. "Let's not imagine a complete break here. A separation is civilized."

"Where is Dad? Is he alright?" Douglas asked.

"I don't know. Probably with Alice happily—"

"Alice the secretary?" Douglas exclaimed.

"Actually," Sally said, "I have spoken to John, and he is doing well, considering the circumstances…" She looked at me. "And he is not with Alice but living in a casita behind his friend Terry's house in the Valley."

"Did he talk about me?" I asked.

"No, Caro, but he did want me to pass on that he will still put money in the household account."

"Too kind, I'm sure."

"Can you please give him a tiniest bit of a break?"

I started to cry.

"Mom! I am sorry Dad has made you so unhappy!" Douglas put his arms around me.

"Oh boys! We've made each other miserable for a long time. And I met someone who I…" I continued to cry.

"That Inspector?" Douglas asked. He saw Max nod his head. "Then you have to do what you have to do, Mom."

"That's what I said," Max agreed.

Silence.

Sally clapped her hands. "OK! This is what's going to happen! You guys will go to school and do your work! Caro! You will go to school and do your work! Keep your bodies healthy! Exercise! Eat organic—"

"Oh please, Sally! We don't need a sermon—" Sally was such a modern day sixties flower child.

"Body, mind, spirit, Sister! Balance! Breath! One must stay strong during times of stress. Eat well!" She got a beatific look on her face. "I remember surviving on *tsampa* hiking the Himalayas. And we were under emotional and physical stress in Nepal. We never knew what was going to appear or happen!"

Max and Douglas stared at her. "What's *tsampa*, Aunt Sally?" they both spoke at the same time.

I sighed. Here we go, I thought.

"*Tsampa* was the food that sustained us on our long days going up and up into the cold mountains! The Nepalese people set up big pots of barley and boiling pots of bark tea with salt and yak butter in front of their homes."

"Ugh!" Max said.

"No! Listen! So you got a bowl of barley and then filled it up with the tea and mashed it together with your hand into a dough ball and ate it! It filled us up and kept us warm all day!"

"That's all you ate?" Douglas asked.

"We also had stinging nettles soup." The boys' eyes glazed over, and I forgot everything in my life. "My point is that one must have good nutrition to deal with difficult times." She picked up a bit of taco shell and dropped it back on her plate.

Max got up and kissed his Aunt. "Have to do homework."

I coughed.

Douglas hugged Sally. "Percussion Ensemble rehearsal!" Then he looked at me. "Are you going to be alright tonight?"

"Yes, honey. Aunt Sally will be here for a while."

"And me!" Max said.

"Love you!" Sally said as they left the kitchen. Then she turned to me. "Now what?"

"We're going to make a goad."

"What?"

"A long pointed stick on two wheels. It rolls out from off stage and pokes the sacks causing the actors to crawl out and start their day."

Sally hugged me. "Oh Caro! Why do you do the things you do?"

"I'm bored?"

Chapter 32

I flipped on the light in the double garage. Sally walked past me, put her hands on her hips, and surveyed tool boxes, bicycles, gardening tools, power tools, work bench, bags of old clothes, rejected art leaning against a wall, cleaning supplies, mops, brooms... a closet.

"Well! What's in the closet?"

"Suitcases, my wedding dress, card table and chairs, paint, humidifiers, down comfort –"

"Do you have any twirly-gig suitcases?"

"Yes. One. I hate it."

"Oh goody," Sally charged into the walk-in closet. I heard all this banging around. She came out smiling and pulling a battered suitcase on wheels. "The goad has wheels!" she exclaimed.

From a very young age my sister loved nothing better than a project. While I was Little Miss Priss playing with dolls and reading Nancy Drew, Sally was building cities with erector sets and setting off stink bombs with her chemistry sets.

I stood like a statue while she rummaged through John's tools. She was on a mission. I stayed out of her way. Music blasted out of the stereo speakers. The garage doors opened.

Max came in. "Thought you'd like some Vampire Weekend and fresh air! What can I do?"

"Take the head off one of those mops," Sally said while she was removing the wheels from the suitcase with a screwdriver. "Find me some duct tape, Caro."

I started going through John's workbench drawers. I felt good actually doing something useful. Not thinking and worrying and wondering and doubting.

Then a big black car pulled into our driveway shining bright headlights into the open garage. My Inspector got out. My sister stopped unscrewing wheels, Max stopped wrestling with a mop, and I held a huge roll of duct tape to my chest. We were quite the tableau. We stared at him. He stared at us.

"What's wrong?" I asked.

"What?" James yelled over the music.

"Please turn off that music, Max!" Max dropped the mop and ran into the house.

Silence.

"What's wrong?" I repeated. Sally walked over and put her arm around me. Max returned and came to my side.

"Nothing. I've been trying to call your cell for an hour. I even called your home line. I was worried."

"My phone is charging in the house. Can't hear the land line out in the garage… I'm OK."

Murder at Theatre X

"Yeah. She's OK," Max said.

James looked at Max. "Good." He turned to me. "I read the professor's autopsy report."

"Let me guess: Death by separation of the head from the body!" Max held up the detached mop head of yarn.

"Actually Richard Smith was poisoned. His head was cut off post-mortem."

"Adding insult to injury," Max said.

"Explains the small amount of blood in Theatre X."

Sally sighed and sat down by the suitcase. Max rubbed the bottom of the mop stick with sand paper. I tried to loosen the end of the duct tape with a finger-nail. I could not muster up excitement about this infor-mation. I seemed to have lost all interest in murder. Was that possible? I still felt peevish over James's lack of praise for my recycling lead.

"I thought you'd like to know," James said.

"Great." I continued picking at the roll of tape.

Silence.

"What are you all doing?"

"We're making a goad," I said.

"OK. Of course...for *Act Without Words II.* Where's John?"

"He's out."

"Let me help."

"That stick needs a point on the end," Sally said.

"Do you have a belt sander?" James started searching through the power tools lined up on shelves. He found one, Max held out the mop handle, James plugged in the sander, ran in over the rod until there was a smooth,

Christina Squire

dull, arrow-like point on the end. Sally brought over two little suitcase wheels. I held out the duct tape with scissors.

"Now one wheel is in the middle and the other is almost at the end."

Sally taped the wheels onto the pointed stick as James held it steady for her.

"Now we paint!" Sally said. "What color do you want?"

"Beckett doesn't say," I said.

"Black!" Max said. Sally bolted into the closet, banged around again, and came out with a can of black paint. I found brushes hanging over the workbench.

Later, we all stood around proudly admiring our masterpiece: The black, rather sinister, goad up on its wheels drying on sheets of newspaper. A car pulled into the driveway.

"Dad's here," Max said.

Chapter 33

John stood at the entrance to the garage. We looked at him. He looked at us. Another tableau. I should be in the Dramatic Writing Program.

"We built a goad, John!" Sally finally said.

"Wow," John said.

"Hello, John," James said.

I was speechless.

John walked quickly to his workbench. He picked up a hammer. He stalked out without a word or a glance in our direction.

Suddenly I was furious. "Where are you going with that hammer?" I yelled. I saw red. Not that he took the damn hammer. I did not care about the damn hammer. I was mad. Irrationally? Perhaps. But perhaps not! Why did I doubt myself seconds after having an authentic feeling?

John stopped but did not turn around. "I am going back to the casita where I live now." He enunciated every syllable like he was talking to a two year old.

"Terry doesn't have a hammer?" I screeched.

"Mom!" Max said.

John faced me. "He is not at home." Taking a tone like I was an idiot.

"Oh, really!" I sneered. We were playing our parts very well.

"Something break, John?" James asked.

"You can say that." John and I glared at each other a long time before he got in his car, slammed the door and left.

I threw the duct tape against a wall.

Silence.

"Well!" my sister exclaimed. "We have gotten a lot done tonight, because we cooperated! I'm proud of us!"

"Thank you all," I said. My voice shook.

"So who is going to operate the goad, Mom?" Max asked as he picked up the tape and put it back in a drawer.

"I don't know..." I sighed.

"Let me, Mom!"

"OK. But you have to attend all the rehearsals, and –"

"I will!"

"Can I be an understudy?" James asked.

"I'm sure!" Max laughed and looked at me.

I stared at the concrete floor. I should have invited everyone in for a drink, but I was mentally, physically and emotionally exhausted. Screaming. I had never screamed before in my marriage. I grew up with a rageaholic father. He screamed at my mother all the time. Screamed and screamed. Did he ever think of his three children shaking in bed with their heads under the pillows? No! When I got married I vowed never to scream at my husband. I swallowed anger. My children never had to go through what I did. But...this behavior weakened me. And what did it teach my sons? Perhaps there was a time for screaming. I was honest for the first time in my married life. Expressing anger dissolved age-old emotional filters and fears. I felt the thick crust of control that had encased my body for years shatter into dust and float away. I was light.

Sally broke the silence. "Max, let's go clean up the kitchen." They left.

James stood next to me.

"You all right?" James said.

"Yes."

"Then please teach me how to use a goad."

Christina Squire

Chapter 34

I texted my actors. I had reserved an empty classroom in the Theatre basement for a rehearsal the next night. They both replied that they could come. I planned to have them practice getting in and out of the sacks. No goad action.

Now what? I was still angry with John for barging into the garage for a hammer, of all things. I wondered if he really needed a hammer but saw James and had to quickly make up some excuse. Maybe he wanted to talk to me. At least he wasn't living with Alice. I was pleased but still mad.

I had to get my mind off garage drama. I hauled the pile of Theatre Appreciation essay exams into the bedroom. I made a pot of coffee, got in bed with my dog, and read bluebooks. I could not read some of the handwriting. I guess schools don't stress cursive anymore. Sam can deal with the chicken scratch ones.

After midnight I finished grading and thought about James. He offered to take me somewhere to talk. I said no. I wondered if I ever wanted conversation from him. We had never really just talked before. Except about murder. Oh I really felt important, needed, happy and helpful sharing information with him. I was so eager to please. And his very presence set every cell in my body on fire. But I was tired of all that right now. I was just tired, period. I turned out the light.

But I kept thinking. Was I tired of murder? Inconceivable! And...Was James just a romantic fantasy for me? Or was he a real flesh and blood human being with strengths and weaknesses? With wants and needs? Did I want to deal with reality? Or reside in a cloud of unknowing?

I tossed and turned. Suki hopped off the bed in a huff. I followed her into the kitchen, gave her a few Milk Bones, poured myself a glass of wine, and grabbed a bag of Doritos. We both jumped back on the bed. Now for some true relaxation! I started reading *The Wit and Wisdom of Oscar Wilde*.

Chapter 35

The next day I watched *Metropolis* in one class, practiced scenes from *The Bald Soprano* in another, and returned the graded tests to Sam and assisted in Theatre Appreciation. I walked across Central for a fiesta burger at the Frontier. I picked up the coffee sacks in the trunk of my Beetle. I was NOT going to leave them in the Theatre X prop room! John had paid a semester fee of $250 for a reserved parking place located in the back of the Fine Arts Building. The sticker came in the mail yesterday. I must thank him sometime.

I met Clarence leaving the main office as I went down to the basement. He had his gym bag. Going to work out as usual, I thought.

"Watch out. Louise is on a tear," he said.

"What's up?"

"She heard something," he answered. "Stay out of her way."

What else is new, I grumped.

I was early. A class was still in session in the room I had reserved. I sat down in the hallway with my sacks and copies of the play. I saw Louise charging down the

107

hall toward me. I braced myself, but she passed by to Professor Smith's office without a glance. Whew. She yanked open the door and yelled "Get out!"

"What?" a female voice said.

"You can't be in here."

"I am in the middle of a read through of my play."

"Take your actors and read in the foyer."

Then I saw Brianne tower over Louise. "I am not going to read in the foyer."

"Step away from me, Brianne. And go. Now." Louise tried to enter the office.

Brianne blocked her. "No one is using this office now! My actors have made this time to read the final version of my play –"

Louise pushed Brianne aside. "All right everyone. Out."

I heard mumbling. Then five students shuffled out. Louise patted each one on the back as they passed by. "Thank you," she said.

"I'll meet you up by Rodey Theatre," Brianne told her actors. Then turned to Louise. "You are a piece of work, Madam Chair!"

"You better watch yourself, Brianne. Give me the key!"

Brianne stared her down. "I don't have a key. The custodian let me in."

Louise pulled out her cell phone. "I'm reporting him. And calling security."

Brianne started laughing. "You know what Richard used to call you? A Popinjay. All strutting around and self-important. All powerful in this third rate department in a third rate university. You were like a mosquito to him. Buzzing around waiting to be slapped."

"Leave, Brianne."

I made a big deal of flipping through Beckett's script, smoothing out my bags, and pretending to care about what was new on my phone. Those two women have a history, I thought. Out of the corner of my eye, I saw Brianne slowly walk away.

She stopped and turned around. "Happy?" Brianne asked.

"I won't be until May when you graduate and are out of my sight."

"Then I've got lots of time!"

"Just remember you don't have your sugar daddy around to protect you anymore." Louise went into Richard's office and slammed the door.

"And you can keep your job," Brianne shouted.

She winked at me on her way down the hallway.

Brianne had recovered quickly from Richard's death. Not the swooning, morose grieving fox but a sleek, bold, clever creature. Did Richard want to be Chair?

Christina Squire

Chapter 36

The young men had fun getting in and out of the sacks. I told them they could not giggle during the performance! Even though this short play was filled with Beckett's black humor, they had to take their parts seriously: Depicting mankind's day to day mind-numbing routines. Choose to be happy or sad. We agreed on another rehearsal time. I'd bring carrots to chew, watches to check the time, and toothbrushes. I asked Bill and Alan to find a worn pair of pants and a beat-up pair of boots that could fit both of them. I'll bring one of John's old hats. I gathered up my bags. Sam said I could store them and all my props in his office.

I walked down the hall. I heard Spanish language and music coming from Theatre X. The doors were open, so I peeked in. There was a huge video screen showing a lovely woman walking on top of a mountain. I blinked my eyes. That was Isabel. And I knew that place! It was *Cola de Caballo* in Monterrey, Mexico. As the camera scanned the area I saw the waterfall, the Hotel Hacienda, and people riding horses and donkeys.

Then the camera panned to unsmiling young girls dressed in rags walking alone on the side of the road. Quite a contrast in subject matter.

My family took a trip to Monterrey years ago. I still had a picture of my mother on a donkey. The poor little beast! My mother's legs were almost touching the ground! At first she did not want to get on that little donkey! "Do not worry, *Señora*! She is strong!" the keeper said. "*Arriba, Arriba, Señora!*"

My brother, sister and I chose placid donkeys instead of a horse. We were not a horse family. My Dad sat on a picnic table and smoked. Driving up the narrow, two lane curving road while honking drivers careened down the mountain about done him in.

A man narrated the video in Spanish. Vincente and Xavier played guitars while Isabel beautifully danced in front of the screen.

I took a seat in Theatre X. I saw the back of a woman sitting in the front row taking notes.

Isabel stopped dancing. The guitarists stopped. She yelled up at the sound booth. "Let's stop!" The screen went blank. Stage lights came on. She walked over to the woman taking notes. But she saw me.

"Caro! Hello!" I stood up to greet her. She gave me a hug. Dancers! So affectionate! And she barely knew me.

"Hope you don't mind, Isabel! I was rehearsing down the hall and—"

"Of course not! You are welcome to watch anytime! I am rehearsing my MFA Project. Agh!"

"Quite a production! Beautiful scenery! And your lovely dance!"

"Yes. I'm calling it *Transitos Abandonados*, Abandoned Transits. I hope to present the journey between a body of memories and the body being present. And how cultural memory lives in geography... It's a work in progress...," she sighed.

"Like all art, Isabel. I'm very impressed so far," I said.

"Thank you, Caro. I was born in Monterrey, and—"

"You look familiar!" The woman from the front row stood next to Isabel. She puffed away on an electronic cigarette.

She was Professor Smith's wife.

"So you know Marnie?" Isabel asked.

"We passed each other in the hall a while ago. We've never actually met. I'm Caro."

Marnie blew a stream of vapor out the side of her mouth. I smelled pineapple. "How will you ever survive grad school without your advisor, Caro?"

"Professor Block is helping me." I did not express sympathy. I did not want to go there.

"Marnie is translating Garcia Lorca's poetry into English for subtitles that will run under the video," Isabel said.

"Wonderful," I said.

"And isn't it just wonderful that my sister and I both married bastards?" a voice purred. I watched Olive step down out of the dark top row of seats and onto the stage.

113

Christina Squire

Chapter 37

My blood ran cold. My heart started to pound. But Olive could never know how shocked I was. Acting. I took several deep breaths.

"Hello, Olive," I said.

"You know Marnie's sister, too?" Isabel exclaimed.

"Yes."

Olive put her long, wiry arm around my shoulders. Her Joy perfume almost made me gag. I swallowed, tried to shrug her arm off and step away from her. She held me close like a vise. "Caro and I go way back, don't we?"

Marnie invaded my space. "Don't tell me this is Caroline Steele!"

"The one and only," Olive said.

As sisters the only thing they had in common were hard, thin mouths, hazel eyes and ropey necks. Marnie was short, pear shaped, fresh faced, with dyed black hair (too black!) in a blunt cut with bangs. She wore baggy clothes like the ones I first saw her wear in the hallway with her mother (probably Chico's, I thought unkindly). The puce color and large, ugly

115

amber necklace did nothing for her sallow complexion. Olive, of course, was resplendent in a denim jumpsuit, tall, thin, expertly made up, platinum hair done in her signature French Roll, sans chopsticks, thank goodness. The ruby eyes in her skull ring flashed.

Xavier called to Isabel. "We need to get back to practice! We only have 30 more minutes reserved in the X."

Isabel turned to us. "Well! What a small world, *si*? Back to rehearsal. Thank you for your comments, Caro. And we'll just rehearse a *cante jondo* without the video, Marnie. You all can catch up!"

The sisters smiled at Isabel. I had no desire to catch up with those two! I had to get out of there. But when Isabel turned her back to talk to the guitarists, they roughly shoved me out of Theatre X and shut the sound proof doors.

"You and your vigilante cop lover framed my sister!" Marnie hissed in my face spraying spit.

"Like Hell we did! Your sister tried to have me killed twice! She murdered a man! Get away from me!" I pushed her. She fell backwards, came down hard on her ass and screamed. Olive dug her talons into my neck. I reached behind, grabbed her shellacked French roll and yanked with all my might.

"You bitch!" Olive yelled and let me go. I started to run. They both came after me. I was trapped against a wall.

"Get away from her, Olive!" My Inspector and Max stood at the end of the hallway. James was holding the goad. I almost laughed with nerves and relief. There

Murder at Theatre X

he was dressed like a Tom Ford model holding this long black pointed rod with two stupid twirling wheels. Max was at his side in a Foo Fighters tee shirt. What a vision!

Marnie and Olive froze.

In three long strides James reached me, lifted me up with one arm, and slightly staggered as he half carried half dragged me to a safe distance. Max took the goad.

"So this is Olive," Max said.

"And YOU are?" Olive asked as she slowly walked towards him. Her loosened French Roll swayed back and forth like a silver snake.

"I am Maximilian Steele."

"Aren't you cute," Olive said.

"Aren't you a hot mess," Max said.

Olive burst out in raucous laughter. "I like you."

"Leave him alone!" I rubbed my neck where she had dug her nails into me. I was bleeding. I probably needed a tetanus shot!

"Your parole officer will hear about this, Olive," James said. He handed me his handkerchief.

"Go ahead! My sister and I were talking to your deluded Caro and," she looked at Max, "your faithful mother, about Mexico, weren't we Marnie? She attacked us! My sister probably has a broken tailbone. Caro pulled my hair and wrenched my neck! She's mental. But you're attracted to those types, aren't you Inspector Hutchinson? Easier to control. Is your wife still in the Swiss sanatorium?"

"Shut it you lying piece of shit!" I screamed. "I am so tired of you!" Max put his arm around me.

117

"Who will they believe? You and your corrupt inspector or me and my poor grieving widowed sister? Come on, Marnie. I'll drive us to the Emergency Room. I think I have whip lash, and I feel a migraine coming on." She whacked the goad with the back of her hand as she passed. "I'm going to press charges!"

Chapter 38

"Mom!"

"Caro!"

My legs gave out. I slumped down to the ground and leaned against the wall like a rag doll. Olive freaked me out again. James and Max knelt down next to me.

"Max, can you get some water?" James said.

Max jumped up. "I think the Satellite kiosk is still open for a Popejoy Event." He ran up the stairs to the foyer.

I took James's hand, kissed it, and pressed it over my heart. "Why…how…you both…here?"

"I saw Max getting off the bus in front of the Frontier Restaurant carrying the goad. He got a lot of stares from people sitting in the window booths!"

He made me laugh. "I can imagine…Why were you near the Frontier?"

James sighed. "I was walking to the Fine Arts Center. I heard Olive was here."

"How?"

James gently removed his hand from my clammy grip and wrapped his arm around me. "A private investigator."

"What?"

"I hired her to follow Olive. And I gave her a picture of you—"

"How did you get a picture of me?"

"Max."

"Talking about me?" Max held three plastic glasses of water.

"Thanks, honey."

We sat against the wall and drank.

"Maggie also told me that she saw you," James said.

"Did she now." I gave him a dreamy look. But I was dizzy.

"And I thought you needed the goad for rehearsal tonight, Mom! I took the Central bus, and everyone ignored me! Like all normal passengers carry goads!"

"Nothing normal about the Central bus riders," I said.

Isabel, Vincente and Joaquin came out of Theatre X. Isabel brought my sacks and purse.

"Oh thank you so much!" I said. We all stood.

"Did you have a nice talk with Marnie and her sister?" she asked me.

"So very nice!"

"*Buenas noches,*" she said.

"*Buenas noches,*" we replied.

Vincente and Xavier glared at my Inspector as they walked away.

Chapter 39

"I'm going to store all my props in Sam's office," I said.

I unlocked the door and turned on the light. Max stood the goad up against the wall between the couch and a file cabinet. I folded the bags and tucked them beside the low, lumpy purple velour sofa. This gaudy piece of furniture horrified Sam when he moved in, but no one came to get it after numerous calls and complaints to Louise. He did drape a pretty indigo woven fringed throw over the back. And he put files and stacks of paperwork on top of the worn cushions.

We were ready to go when James said, "I still have to talk to your Mother about Professor Smith's murder, Max."

I was ready to talk about murder again. And I had some information for him. I was goaded! I was excited once more.

"Here are my car keys, Max. James can bring me home. Right, James?"

"Of course."

"OK, Mom." We hugged each other. "I'm so sorry you had to go through this."

121

"Me, too, but no one got seriously hurt. I'm thankful."

"Will Olive really bring charges against you?"

"Nothing will come of her wild threats, Max," James said. "She better not call any attention to herself if she knows what's good for her. While her case is under appeal, she has to live like a monk. Or pretend to."

"See you later, honey. Drive carefully."

I shut the door. James came behind me. He put his hands gently on my shoulders.

"How are you?" he asked.

My eyes filled with tears. I so had many worries and doubts. I took a deep breath. We could get a coffee upstairs, come back down here, sit on the funky couch and honestly talk. About what a huge change it was in my life for John to leave, how this may affect my children, what really happened in New Orleans, and did he love his wife.

But then…irrationally…

I locked the door, turned around and grabbed his hair. We kissed passionately. We stumbled over to the purple couch locked together.

"Where's Sam?" James whispered against my lips.

"Daughter's school…Spaghetti Night," I said.

James let me go. While he moved stacks of paper off the cushions onto Sam's desk, I lifted the black Target tunic over my head and tossed it into the air, kicked off my Sketchers and peeled off my striped Old Navy tights. James threw me on the couch. I sucked my finger while he tore off his plaid shirt and chinos. I was on fire. He slowly lowered himself over me. I put my finger in his mouth. He bit. A charge went through my body. Then

Murder at Theatre X

he laced his fingers through mine and kissed me over and over again. I wound my legs tightly around him. I could never get enough of his kiss.

Or anything else.

Christina Squire

Chapter 40

I leaned against the couch armrest searching through my purse. James got up to get something out of his pants pocket, covered me with the indigo throw, and sat down. I tucked my feet under him. I found a mandarin orange and peeled it slowly, breathing in the burst of fresh aroma. I felt fresh.

"So Maggie the Private Eye?" I asked.

"I have to keep track of Olive. And I am very worried about you."

"Thank you, James." He does care, I thought. He stayed with me in the hospital. He said he moved here because of me. But who was he really? How long could we go on like this: A wonderful, exhilarating, passionate "this"? Why do I question every honest emotion I have? And every action I take? Expressing anger or passion? Were they two sides of the same coin? And I was giving voice to both for the first time in my life. I must trust my feelings and stop second guessing myself. I was happy now. And here is now, as the Yogis say.

I finally tuned in to James who was talking like a policeman.

"...and Olive has her lawyers spying on us," he was saying.

"Spy versus spy!" I laughed. I fed him a few sections of fruit. "Olive's crazy. So is her sister! No wonder the professor left her for the Fox!"

"I never told you what we found with his head." James said. "And," he held my hand, "I never thanked you for that crucial lead. Good work, Caro."

About time, I thought! But I said, "Thank you... what did you find?"

"A note. I made a copy." He read: "*Vimos demasiado. Escuchamos demasiado. Cierra la boca.*"

"I only understood close your mouth."

James translated: "We saw too much. We heard too much. Shut up." He paused. "My maternal grandmother was Spanish."

"Oh? Mine was Macedonian."

"Oh?"

"*Se topli*"

"I'll take that as a compliment."

"You wish!" I threw some rind at him.

"Moving right along," James said as he tossed the rind in the trash can, "---and I will Google Translate that---Mexican drug gangs decapitate rival gang members and often leave notes next to the heads."

"I can't believe Richard was into drugs," I said.

"He must have been into something illegal..." James started rubbing my feet. He was good at that, too. "The way he was baiting you to act in some movies and make a lot of money was a red flag."

"Totally inappropriate."

Murder at Theatre X

"There is a way to find out if he was involved with pornography," he said.

"I'm sure you know some links."

"I investigate, Mrs. Steele."

"Don't I know..." I reluctantly moved my feet away from his magic fingers, stood up, wrapped the throw around me, and sat at Sam's desk. I was ready to get serious about murder, "Have you checked alibis?"

"Of course." James put on his pants.

"Well?"

"I need coffee first." He buttoned up his shirt and put on his shoes without socks.

"I take cream," I said as he went out the door.

"I know!"

I walked around nude feeling light and free. I checked out Sam's bookshelf. Lots of Performance Theory. I never associated theory with theatre, but I may learn something in graduate school. What a concept!

My phone beeped. I got a text: 'Jane Keyes is joining us for coffee.'

Christina Squire

Chapter 42

Damn! I moved fast! I looked wildly around for the clothes that I had thrown with such abandon. I found my tunic, slipped it over my head, picked up my tights in a corner, sat down and struggled to pull them on, found one shoe. Oh I'll just go barefoot! I pushed the single shoe under the couch. I draped the indigo blanket neatly over the back cushions. I smoothed my hair. Done! I thought! I heard voices coming down the hall! I took a deep breath. Put on my huge black reading glasses. I picked up one of Sam's books and sat at his desk. I hoped to exude a scholarly air.

Who was I trying to fool? I took off my glasses and put down the book. I stood up.

My tunic was on inside out.

The door opened.

My Inspector held the door for Jane to enter. He followed carrying three large coffees on a tray.

"Hello, Caro," Jane said.

"Hi, Jane."

"Let's have a seat," James said. I sat back down at Sam's desk. James handed me a coffee. They sat on the sofa.

Silence. Jane sipped her coffee and looked around. She looked all neat and crisp in black slacks, white shirt, short blonde hair, and shiny black Doc Marten boots. I was sweating under my armpits. Now that I wasn't rushing around like a maniac, I noticed my missing shoe leaning against Sam's hard drive and my Inspector's socks on the floor. Whatever.

"Heard you had quite a night, Caro," she said. "Marnie and Olive were at the UNM Police Station filing an assault and battery complaint against you."

"The nerve!" I exclaimed.

"James filled me in on what happened. But I have to talk to you…procedure."

"They attacked me. I defended myself. Period."

Jane said. "I believe you."

"Thanks ever so," I said.

Jane turned to my Inspector. "I want to talk to Caro alone."

"Sure," James said. "Text me when you're done. I'm driving her home."

Oh! He's leaving me with her!

"I'll drive her home," Jane said.

They were talking about me like I wasn't even there! "Excuse me! No one will drive me home! I'll call Uber." I turned to Jane. "I'll give you ten minutes."

"Please calm down, Caro," Jane said.

James said, "I'll be in the foyer if you both need me…" He saw the looks on our faces. "You probably won't," he added and left.

"What happened?" Jane asked.

Chapter 43

"What happened when?" I asked.

"When you were with Marnie and Olive in the hallway, of course!"

"Oh that. I was watching a rehearsal in Theatre X. Marnie and Olive were there. They muscled me out into the hallway. Marnie screamed in my face, said I framed her sister, I pushed her away, and her plump body fell down. Olive dug her nails into me. I pulled her hair to make her stop."

I stretched the neckline of my tunic down to show her the wounds.

"Ugh. Ugly," Jane said. Then: "The Target label is on the outside of your top."

"It's the new style." As if Jane didn't know that I had put this on in a panic when I heard she was coming!

"It is?" She was being sly. She knew it and knew I knew it.

We laughed a nervous laugh and sat on the lumpy sofa.

Silence.

"Any witnesses?" she asked.

"No." I sighed. I looked at my watch. "Yeah…well… that's what happened." I started to feel uncomfortable and got up. I continued to imagine she disapproved of my relationship with James. Why did I care what she thought? Maybe I was still uncertain…

"I'm worried about you, Caro," Jane said. "Please sit down."

"What?" I sat.

"Olive is a psychopath. She is out to do you and James harm."

"Hmmm." Yes, Jane, I knew she had someone stab me with a knife. Then Olive almost stabbed me in the eye with a chopstick while I was in the hospital. I still experienced instant recall of her cloying Joy perfume as she bent over me. I knew she was dangerous, but I thought she would keep a low profile awaiting her trial. After tonight I realized this was not true. I was living under a false sense of security.

"I wouldn't be surprised if she was involved in the professor's murder---for her sister's sake. It's her recreation."

"Do they have alibis?"

"They were at the movie with their mother the night before Richard was found."

But, I thought, he was poisoned. Who knows? One or all of those vixens could have killed him any time. I stood up. "I'll watch my back, Jane."

She took my hand and gently pulled me back down on the sofa. "I'm not done. James has already hired Maggie to follow Olive. But she is a very clever woman. You have to be aware of your surroundings. I can arrange to have a police escort with you at all times when you're on campus. And now that you're living alone—"

"Word travels fast, doesn't it?" James! "Two of my sons live at home. I have a dog. I am not alone." But I started to worry. Olive may harm my children and kill my dog. Horrible woman! I got up again and gathered the files and paperwork on Sam's desk. I started to stack them neatly back on the cushions. But I did not want an escort watching my every move: Moves that may involve my Inspector. And reporting back to Jane. "An escort will interfere with my creative process," I said.

"The escort could sit outside the room you are in." Jane stood. "And Max and Douglas are probably gone a lot with their activities—"

"I can take care of myself! Your ten minutes are over!" I had enough of her advice. She was scaring me. I picked up James's socks and stuffed them in my purse. I pulled one shoe out from under the couch and got the other one by the hard drive. I put the coffee cups in the trash on top of the mandarin rinds and Kind bar wrapper. Sam will think a party was going on in here. Well…

"Please don't get on the defensive with me. I am on your side! I don't think you and James realize how much danger you both are—"

"It's James, isn't it?"

"What?"

"You're more worried about James, aren't you? You told me to stay away from him. I know why. I'm not stupid." I accidently hit the goad propped up on the

133

side of the couch when I forcefully picked up my purse. It clattered to the floor. Jane picked it up. She aimed the point at me.

"I care about both of you." She leaned the goad back against the wall. Her phone rang. She went out in the hall. But I could still hear: "I'm OK. Are you home? I'm still with Caro. Mumble. Mumble…as soon as… mumble." Frustrating! I put my ear against the door. "Love you, too, Maggie."

(A supervisor once who told me: "Never assume. It makes an ass out of you and me.")

"I'm an ass!" I announced when Jane came back in the office.

Jane laughed a true laugh. "Oh Caro! Please! Where did that come from? You are so funny!"

Chapter 44

We pulled up in front of my house in her unmarked police car.

"Thank you, Jane," I said. "Want to come in for an adult beverage?"

"Well…" She looked at her watch. "I am off duty now. Thanks."

Max and Douglas came running out the front door. "What's wrong?" Douglas shouted.

"What happened?" Max yelled.

"Nothing! I'm fine!" I said. They hugged me tightly. "Lt. Keyes gave me a ride home, that's all." I introduced them.

Suki rushed to greet me in the house. Jane pet her. "I love dogs. We can't have pets where we live."

"Why are your clothes inside out, Mom?" Max asked.

"I've been too distracted, I guess. It's supposed to be good luck!" I said merrily.

"They weren't inside out in the hallway," he said.

Oh that boy! "Hey! It's garbage night. Can you guys please move the bins to the curb for pick-up tomorrow morning?"

135

Max gave me a big smile then followed Douglas to the garage.

"He is very observant like his mother," Jane smiled.

"Max will do me in yet!"

Jane and I walked into the kitchen. "Wine, beer, vodka…?"

"I'll have some white wine. Your sons are very handsome, Caro."

"Thank you. My eldest is in Austin going to the University of Texas."

"You must be so proud of them."

"I am. My finest accomplishments."

I put some happy hard salami from Sprouts, provolone, and crackers on a plate. I added a cluster of red grapes.

We sat in the den with our healthy glasses of wine. I could hear music coming from behind my sons' doors. But they had turned it down to a low roar.

"Your home is so colorful and uncluttered," Jane said.

"Feng Shui. My husband John and I at least agreed on design. Something."

"I hope things work out for you."

"Yeah…well…Thank you."

She took a sip of wine. "James has marital issues, too."

I drained my glass. "I know."

"He's crazy about you, Caro."

My eyes filled with tears. I got up. "We need napkins." I went in the kitchen. I was emotionally overwhelmed. I stood at the sink. Jane came by side.

"I didn't mean to upset you," she said.

"No…no…you didn't.   What you said made me happy! I was never sure, you see. I often thought he was playing with me."

"Not from what I've heard…are you playing with him?"

"No!"

"Good. I don't want to see him hurt. He's has enough problems."

"Like what? Aside from his wife being in a sanatorium?"

"It's not for me to say."

Once again I felt the familiar feeling of resentment towards Jane. My Inspector confided in her. He trusted her. Not me. But did I trust him? Did I tell him about my deepest fears and tragic losses? No. Did trust trump sex? Trust is a form of intimacy. But I had to trust him to give myself to him, didn't I? All I knew was at times I could not breathe unless I had him in my arms.

I pulled a few napkins out of the holder. I blew my nose in one. I grabbed the bottle of wine. "Can we talk about murder now?"

"You're in the wrong profession, Caro."

"All the world's a stage," I said.

Christina Squire

Chapter 45

"James told me about the note in Spanish left by the professor's head," I said as we returned in the den.

"Awful."

"Isabel, the flamenco dancer and her guitarists, are from Mexico. She had that scream fest with the professor," I said.

"They were rehearsing until midnight in Carlisle Gym."

"Marnie is bilingual...but so are most New Mexicans...wish I were."

"She said that she was having family night at the movies."

"Yeah, that's right. But those women could all be in a David Lynch movie." I sat back on the $3,000 couch. Suki was stretched out between Jane and me. "I saw a snit fit between Louise, the Chair, and Brianne tonight."

"Oh?"

Jane ate a few grapes while I stuffed myself with salami and cheese layered high on salty crackers. No wonder she stayed so slim.

139

Christina Squire

"Louise kicked Brianne and her cast out of the professor's office. Brianne told her that she is probably very happy that she can keep her job now that Richard was dead."

"I don't think keeping your job as chair of a small department is a strong enough motive to cut someone's head off. Louise told me she was at a play until ten that night and then went to a cast party. And Brianne said she was having a mani-pedi, haircut and color job at her daughter Zoe's salon."

"Did you question Clarence? He's always got his ear to the ground," I asked. I refilled our glasses.

"He was the last person to see Richard alive. He said a package came for Richard just as he was leaving the office at five. Clarence brought it down to him on his way out to have dinner with his mother on the West Side and spent the night."

"I wonder what was in that package, and where was it from?" I finally took a grape.

"My questions, too. We searched Richard's home, car, office...never found anything." She put her full glass of wine down.

"Maybe it was recycled?" I said.

Jane laughed. "You're probably right again!"

"I can't stop thinking about the creepy way Richard suggested I act in films for a lot of money. Was he involved in porn? Could that be what the note was referring to? Seeing too much? Hearing too much?"

"That's a good lead, Caro. We'll look into that...But I should go. Before I do I want to thank you for your help. You are observant. People confide in you. And you take chances. But you almost died last year. Be careful! Think about an escort! Please tell us when you discover evidence. James and I will follow through. Trust us. Promise?"

"I promise."

I crossed my fingers under the inside out tunic.

Christina Squire

Chapter 46

After Jane left, I picked up the wine glasses, and stuffed the rest of the food on the snack plate in my mouth. I thought about how shallow (or mercenary!) I was to befriend Jane once I knew she was not interested romantically in my Inspector. Well, that was the reality of the situation. I was letting my bad self emerge. And embracing it. But I did have a pleasant time with her. And she really was trying to help. She seemed genuinely compassionate.

I checked on Max and Douglas. They had eaten bags of Taco Bell for dinner and were doing homework with music blaring.

For the first time I locked the screen door as well as the front door.

After my bath I poured another glass of wine and sat out on the back deck with my dog. I lit a ciggie and wondered about James. What were his problems? He always looked healthy. I knew he was in good shape! He was reinstated in the New Orleans Police Department in good standing: cleared of planting evidence. The Albuquerque Police Department hired him, for crying out loud. Did he have demented parents somewhere? Crazy sisters or brothers? OK, his wife slept a lot. Did James cause her exhaustion? Did he drug her? Psychologically abuse her?

I was getting anxious. My imagination was running wild. And then worrying about maniac Olive on top of everything! James and I have to talk, period.

My phone rang. Peter! Calling from Austin wanting to Face Time. My stomach turned over. Was he sick? Fear shot through my body! I put out the cigarette. Peter detested smoking. I pressed accept.

His handsome face filled the screen: black hair, black brows, long black lashes, beautiful hazel eyes…but he was frowning. "What's wrong?" I shouted.

"Mom! You don't have to shout at the phone! Nothing is wrong!"

"Thank God."

"When were you going to tell me Dad left?"

"It just happened this week---so much is going on---I wanted to but—"

"Dad called and told me that you're involved with that Inspector."

"Well, yes—"

"Do you love him?" he asked. Always came directly to the point, that boy. I don't know where he inherited that trait.

"I do." I surprised myself. I did not take time to think.

"Poor Dad!"

"Poor Dad nothing! He's involved with Alice!"

"Alice the secretary?" Peter exclaimed. Now who was shouting at the phone? His raised voice must have caused his girlfriend Leah to appear on screen and wrap her arm around him. We waved.

"Yes," I said.

"Amazing…" Peter tried not to laugh. He pressed his lips together. He shook his head and took a deep breath. "So you love a James William Hutchinson from New Orleans?" Peter continued.

Silence. I nodded. I was so tired. I did not want to go through a third degree.

"Have you Googled him?" he asked.

"No! I've known him for a few years and worked with him and—"

"I've Googled him," Peter's voice got very low. "I don't think you know him that well."

Christina Squire

Chapter 47

I had to move! Adrenalin coursed through my body. I started pacing back and forth in the back yard bathed in moonlight. My shaking hand held the phone up to my face. "What are you trying to say?"

"His first wife Jacqueline was gunned down on the street by a bullet meant for him."

"Oh my God!"

"Their toddler daughter Claire was with them. The report said that James suddenly bent down to pick up his daughter's doll that had fallen in the gutter. A shot rang out. His wife was killed."

I collapsed on the grass and leaned against the English walnut tree. "Horrible."

"Inspector Hutchinson was the lead on breaking up a drug ring that transported heroin from Mexico on barges that ran up and down the Mississippi River from New Orleans. And they probably trafficked Mexican girls. They never found the shooter."

"Oh. Awful." I started to cry. I tore up handfuls of grass. Suki came and laid her head in my lap.

Peter continued to summarize material off his laptop.

147

"But Hutchinson relentlessly continued for years to find and convict those involved with the continuing drug and sex trade. I found articles of raids, pictures of him searching barges, opening sacks of grain, going through piles of scrap metal." Peter scrolled down. "He remarried the socialite Monique Dumas. You can see the wedding pictures on line. They look like movie stars. Claire was seven."

"I know James is married, Peter," I sighed.

"He was convicted of planting heroin in a barge coal storage."

"The charges were dropped."

"Because he discovered two Inner Harbor Navigational Canal authorities were getting cuts from drug money and prostitution by passing the particular barges during routine inspections. The barges were free to continue their journey up north on the Mississippi. They planted the heroin, testified that they saw James do it just to get him off the police force. And… hmmm, hummm," Peter scanned.

My head was spinning. Too much reality.

"Here it is," Peter read. "James traced their cell phone calls to a captain of one of the tugboats that pushed the barges connected with illegal trafficking. A George Buford was charged and convicted with the two Harbor authorities. But they all had solid alibis for the day of the shooting…and then there's this: Inspector Hutchinson vowed to never rest until Jacqueline's murderer was found." Peter closed his laptop with a snap. "There are more articles in *The Times Picayune*, Mom."

I stroked Suki and got up. She followed me to the deck. I collapsed in a chair. "I need to process all this, honey." My ears were ringing.

"And you need to think about a future with this troubled married man," Peter said.

"Thank you, Brother," I said.

"I love you, Mom."

"I love you, too, and miss you."

Christina Squire

Chapter 48

It was time to pray. I was very disturbed after I Face Timed with Peter. I felt so sorry for James. Why didn't I think of Googling him? Probably Olive did. How else could she know about his history in the New Orleans Police Department? But how did she know his wife was in a Swiss sanatorium?

After filling up my Saturday with grocery shopping and studying, I woke up the next morning and walked to church. (I read that a one mile walk was worth a five milligram Valium.) The air felt good on my arms. I felt gratitude for the gift of life itself. But the usual worries and fears pushed those thoughts out of my mind. It was so strange not having John in the house---even if he was an irritant. I was used to feeling irritated. For better or worse it was familiar. I had to substitute another thought pattern. Something positive. Now there was a novel concept!

Max honked as he whizzed by in my Beetle. He was thrilled that I let him have the car all day.

Christina Squire

I was a member of St. Luke's Episcopal Church. My sons grew up there: baptized, confirmed, and active in youth groups. John never went. Now Peter and Douglas had no love for organized religion. Only Max continued to attend. I suspected it was because of the youth group's loosely chaperoned field trips. I always sang in the choir until I got involved with murder and now graduate school. I missed the music and camaraderie of being in a chorus. We were like our own little tribe---separate from church politics. We had a new priest who came from New Orleans several years ago after his home and church were destroyed by Hurricane Katrina. He believed church should be joyful. Now there were potlucks and growlers and dancing to live music celebrating every liturgical holiday.

First I lit a candle at the ye olde New Orleans style (I guess!) grotto in a dark corner of the church. A beautiful icon of the Virgin Mary and Child draped in purple cloth hung over the candles. Then I knelt in a pew. No supplications. I just felt peace. For once.

The organ swelled into the processional hymn. The congregation stood. I watched the cross bearer walk majestically down the center aisle by followed by Max and a teenage girl side by side robed in white holding candles: two angelic (looking) acolytes. Then came the choir robed in red, then the colorfully vested Verger and priest. Ritual filled me with wonder. I often disagreed with doctrine, but I loved the way church made me feel.

While singing the Gloria James slid into the pew beside me.

Chapter 49

"Max invited me, remember?" My Inspector said as we passed the peace by shaking hands.

"Well, welcome to St. Luke's!" I gushed like one of the ushers greeting a newcomer.

"I've been coming, Caro. Where have you been?" James said.

"I've been distracted," I said. I turned to give the peace sign up to the choir members who were leaning over the loft balcony rail waving at me. Many parishioners shook James's hand like they knew him. I passed the peace with James again. This time I gave the peace that passed understanding. I put my arms around him. I buried my face in his neck. The church filled with the sounds of people talking and laughing and milling around passing peace all over the place. Quite an uproar for a long time. I did not let James go. Let the church bitties talk!

"Peace be always with you," he whispered in my ear.

The priest started reading announcements. Finally everyone sat down. I held his hand.

After the service was over we filed out slowly (too slowly!) with the congregation. I never liked to mingle

153

and chat after church. Almost all the choir members left immediately after the service by a side door. But I smiled and talked to a few people as we inched forward. People were nice. They missed seeing me in choir. Finally we squeezed through the sanctuary double doors into the foyer.

Father O'Hara stood there greeting, talking and laughing with everyone. He was too happy! I wanted to pass behind him, but James still held my hand. We were next in the receiving line.

"James!" the priest boomed. "So glad to see you! And you brought this lost sheep back into the fold!" He gave me a bear hug. "Caro! When are you coming back to choir?"

"Soon...soon," I said.

"Glad to hear it!" Father O'Hara said and then enthusiastically greeted the next person in line.

James started walking down the narrow hallway to the parlor for coffee hour. I stopped at the door to the parking lot.

"I'm going home," I said.

"Why?" he asked.

"I want to."

"Why?"

I sighed. "I do not go to social hour! I have nothing in common with church people. I have nothing to say. It's not my thing. I have to clean my house."

James laughed. "How strange...this is your church..."

"OK! I'll stay! But not for long!" I put on a happy face and entered the parlor filled with the aroma of freshly brewed coffee. A long table was filled with pastries, deviled eggs, breads, raw vegies, fruit, cheeses, bagels and schmear. People were circling like vultures piling their paper plates high with food.

While James stood in the coffee line, I wandered around looking at the current art exhibit---yet another tradition the new priest started. A tiny older lady approached me. I thought her name was Shirley. She looked like a little bird: bright blue eyes, tiny mouth with red lipstick, round circles of blush on crepey cheeks, bushy short white hair and wearing a little electric blue hat with a white feather.

"So good to see your husband in church!" she chirped. "He's so handsome! I see where that darling boy Max gets his looks! And you were both so affectionate!"

I smiled. "He's not my husband."

Shirley (?) blinked several times. "Oh! Well! Good to see you again, Caro." She scurried away to join a group of ladies of a certain age. I was sure she was telling them all about it.

Father O'Hara came over. "Enjoying our new exhibition?"

"Very much!" I said. Actually I was so over landscapes.

"How long have you known James?" he asked.

"A few years."

"We go back a long time. His family attended my church in New Orleans…." He shook his head. "James has been through—"

James joined us with two coffees. The priest put his arms around us. "God bless you both," he said and left.

Christina Squire

Chapter 50

"You can go now if you want," James said.

"Thanks." He took my coffee. "I'll see you." I walked through the jabbering crowd down the hallway and out the door. Ah! Relief! I guess I was an introvert. I got as far as the street.

"Caro!" My Inspector called. "Wait!" He ran up to me. "What are you doing?"

"I'm walking home!"

"Get in my car."

I looked at the Jeep Commander and laughed. "I don't think that's a good idea after so much praying!" But I jumped in the front seat and shamelessly longed to be in the back seat with him.

He parked in front of my house. We heard drumming from the garage.

"Douglas is practicing. Can you come in for a while? Even with all the noise?"

"I'd love to."

Suki greeted us. James made a fuss over her.

157

"Jane told me she liked your home."

"We had a nice talk," I said as I kicked off my church flats, threw my purse in a chair, and draped my church jacket over the back. "Are you hungry? Or did you graze at church?"

"No grazing. No time. I had to get you out of there."

The loud drumming was vibrating my sternum. Or was it my heart?

"What?" I yelled.

"Hungry!" James yelled.

"Omelet?" I shouted.

"Yes!" he shouted.

James sat at the kitchen table and flipped through the New York Times while I beat eggs, cream, and dill together. Then I plopped down on his lap.

"Ooof," he said.

"Do you eat chili?"

"I love chili."

I started to get up. He pulled me back and kissed me. So good. I could have stayed there all morning. And all day and night. But I had to cook! It was the Macedonian way! Feed your man. Then do other things.

I pulled green chili, Colby cheese, and sliced ham out of the refrigerator. I got two slices of Fano Rustic Loaf bread out of the freezer, buttered them and put them in the toaster oven. I rinsed off happy strawberries from Sprouts. I sliced an avocado.

I found two small bottles of Freixenet sparkling wine. I made mimosas.

The omelet was good even though it exploded when flipped. We ate outside on the deck. The drumming was not as loud. We could hear the birds singing. Suki was stretched out on the grass in the sun.

Silence. James walked around the back yard. Suki pranced beside him. I picked up our dishes and stacked them in the dishwasher. I had to talk to him sometime.

He came in the kitchen. "Your tomatoes still look good. I had a big garden in New Orleans."

"I bet things grew well in that climate!" I suddenly felt awkward. But Douglas came in through the garage.

"Hi Mom!" He saw James. The look on his face changed. "Inspector Hutchinson."

"James, please." James put out his hand.

Douglas looked James up and down. Finally, after what seemed like minutes, he shook his hand. "Ok… James."

"Have you eaten, honey?" I asked. I flushed at Douglas's cold behavior.

"I'm meeting friends at the Frontier. Then rehearsal at the university." He kept staring at James.

"Have fun!" I said. Gaily.

Douglas looked at me. Unsmiling. "I hope you both have fun, too." He turned around quickly and left.

Silence. I felt uncomfortable. James was nonplussed.

I bustled around folding dish towels, wiping down surfaces, straightening newspapers…. James watched me. Like he sensed I had something important to say, but yet I was moving around doing all kinds business. I threw down the sponge. "Let's sit, James."

Christina Squire

Chapter 51

In the den James looked at family photos on the bookshelf and pinned to my bulletin board. "This is Peter?" he asked.

"Yes."

"You have handsome sons."

"Thank you." I collected piles of magazines, books, catalogs and back scratchers off surfaces. "Do you have a picture of Claire?"

James took out his wallet. He pulled out a picture. She had an olive complexion, black short hair, straight dark brows, his green eyes and beautiful mouth. She wore no make-up. She didn't need it. "She's lovely, James," I said.

"She has her mother's coloring." He put her picture back in his wallet and picked up a framed picture on the mantle taken at Easter years ago.

"Now I recognize your sister Sally, you, and John. Who are the rest?" John had set up his camera on a tripod and timed it to take a group photo of my family squeezed together on a small couch. We were all laughing. We were all alive.

"This is my Mom with Peter on her lap and my Dad."
I pointed. "This is my brother David." We had our
arms draped around one another.

"I remember you said he died."

"Drunk driver. My mother was killed by a drunk
driver, too."

"I am so sorry."

I took his hand. "I am sorry for your loss, too."

His eyes narrowed. "Jane told you?"

"No." We sat on the couch. Suki jumped up next to
James. He kept petting her and not looking at me. I
had to tell the truth. "Peter Googled you."

He turned to me. His green eyes grew dark. "I will
carry guilt for Jacqueline's death the rest of my life."

"What happened was awful! But it wasn't your fault!"

James got up. "I can't talk about this."

I stood. "You can't or you won't? So grieve, James!
But you still have a life to live and love to give! You have
a daughter! We must to choose life! And be grateful!"

"I'll be grateful when I watch her murderer put to
death." He walked out of the house.

That went well, I thought, and sighed. I knew where
his passion lay.

I changed into sweat pants and Lucharitos tee shirt and
started to clean the house. I blasted out Buena Vista
Social Club on the stereo. I scrubbed the bathroom
floor on my hands and knees (the Macedonian way). I
sprinkled cleanser inside the toilet and swooshed force-

fully with a bowl brush. I heard Suki bark. Someone at the door! On Sunday?

I answered the door with the dripping brush. James! He stepped in, swept me up in his arms and kissed me passionately.

Should I settle for leftovers? I dropped the brush.

Christina Squire

Chapter 52

When Max came home James and I were in the den. James was stretched out on the couch watching a football game with Suki curled up at his feet. I was in John's Finnish chair preparing a lecture that I was going to give to the Theatre Appreciation class on auditioning. I was feeling quite… content.

"You looked great this morning in church, Max," I said.

"Thanks, Mom. Hi, James." He collapsed in a chair.

"Where have you been?" I asked not expecting the truth.

"Melanie and I drove around. Went to the Botanical Gardens."

"Was Melanie the other acolyte?" James asked.

"Yes…and she moved here from New Orleans, too. She heard about you, James, on the local news."

"Really?" James turned off the TV.

"I can't believe how many people from New Orleans have moved here!" I said.

"Mom! Refugees from Katrina! Anyway, as I was trying say to James, Melanie said that New Orleans is a

165

violent city where even police murder each other. She thinks you must feel very lucky to be alive."

"Max!" I slammed my notebook down on a table. I did not want to continue this conversation. Max looked confused for once in his life. His eyes flicked from me to James.

"It's all right, Caro," James sat up. "Melanie's right, Max. I'm glad to be here."

"So much for that, I guess…" Max glared at me. I glared back. Then he smiled. "So what's for dinner, Mom? Don't say happy chicken!" He went to the kitchen and came back with a coke.

"How about Il Vicino?" James said. "My treat."

"Brilliant! Thank you!" said Max. "I'll pick up!"

James, Douglas, Max and I sat at the round dining room table and ate delicious Salsiccia and Rustica pizzas and spinach salad. We drizzled Il Vicino chili oil on every slice. Douglas was silent, but politely answered James's questions about the university jazz program.

"I went to see Dad today," Max said.

"How is he doing?" I asked. Like I cared. But I did.

"We didn't talk much. I surprised him. He was going fishing with Terry up in the Jemez…He looked good."

"That's nice," I said. I was still so mad at John I could spit. But I refused to waste any energy on him. Not now, at least.

"Alice was there," Max said. "She was barefoot and wearing a kimono."

"Here we go," Douglas said.

"Was the kimono blue with white fish on it?" I asked. My face started to burn.

"Yes," Max said and helped himself to another slice.

"I bought that for him at Gallery One for his birthday last year! And he lets her wear it!"

"How can you be upset?" Douglas asked.

"What's that supposed to mean?" I snapped. But I knew exactly what he meant. I was a hypocrite: Another facet of my emerging dark side. We stared at each other until James spoke.

"I'd like to fish in the Jemez sometime."

"We'll go. It's beautiful up there," Max said. They talked about fishing. I took several deep breaths. Douglas started clearing the table.

I clinked glasses of chianti with James. For now, no more personal questions about his life or mine, because if you dig down too deep, you lose good sleep as Joni Mitchell sang.

"Who wants to play a game?" Max said.

Douglas groaned but joined us.

"Who wants to solve the professor's murder?" I asked.

"Who wants to Google poisons?" James asked.

I ran to get my laptop. "What poison killed Richard?"

"Fentanyl," James said.

"That killed Prince and Michael Jackson," Max said.

"Michael Jackson died of propofol," Douglas said. "A sedative."

"Was Richard taking opioids?" I started typing.

"His doctors did not prescribe it," James said. "He

got it somewhere else or someone gave it to him. The pathologist found no signs of injections, however."

"A puzzlement!" I said.

"Mom!" Douglas said. "Did you read in the news where a policeman handled blocks of powdered fentanyl during a bust, then absent mindedly rubbed his face and immediately went into a coma? If they didn't rush him to the hospital, he would have died!"

James and I looked at each other. This was a new possibility.

"Why don't we have some fun and Google Olive---the ultimate poison?" Max said.

"Yay!" I cried. James laughed.

"Let's see," Max said as he searched. "I'll look under Olive Lowry then Olive Walters...Here's her wedding announcement to poor Charles Lowry...blah...blah... and a picture of her wearing white with black witchy hair. Olive Lorraine nee Montpassent married Charles Lowry...blah... And another announcement of her marrying Roland Walters...yadda...yadda...Olive Walters new owner of Mariposa Gallery...blah... Olive Walters accused of murdering homeless man—" James suddenly got up and went out back. I followed him. He was standing in the middle of the yard staring up at the stars.

"What's wrong?" I asked.

"I knew a Chief Montpassent in New Orleans. He was head of my squadron."

"What are chances of him being related to Olive? Inconceivable! But Olive did know you were accused of planting evidence and that Monique was in a Swiss sanatorium! Oh James! Too much of a coincidence!"

Murder at Theatre X

He grabbed my shoulders. "Is it?"

"Every story, every dream, every waking minute of our lives is filled with one fateful coincidence after another," I whispered---almost to myself.

"What?"

"A Chinese saying. They believe if there is no coincidence, there is no story," I said.

James stared at me. "I have to go."

"James! I—"

He left.

He had a story. And I was not in it.

Christina Squire

Chapter 53

The next morning I parked my car in back of the Fine Arts Center. I clutched my notes for the lecture I was going to give to Theatre Appreciation class. Instead of reviewing them my thoughts turned to James. He was shaken about the possibility that Olive could be related to his former supervisor in the New Orleans police department. As usual, I had recently escaped reality by reading a library book by Lisa See late into the night. *Tea Girl on Hummingbird Lane* was a novel about the Akha mountain tribe of China. I was fascinated by their philosophy about one's life being determined by coincidence. Olive knew too much about James not to think that she had a connection in New Orleans.

I had to deal with this later. I had a full day ahead of me and had to focus on realties not what ifs!

Sam and I went back to his office after Theatre Appreciation ended. I had to get my African Dance clothes. He was so kind to let me store props, books and a change of

171

clothes in his space. He praised my talk on auditioning. I was so nervous, but I guess it went OK. I got some laughs describing my more humiliating experiences: when trying out for *Auntie Mame* I was singing my song in front of the director and others sitting at a long table when the director leaned over, whispered something to the person beside him, and they burst out laughing. Or when I was reading a scene for *Steel Magnolias* and the director threw my resume and headshot on the floor. Another red flag was when I poured my heart out reciting Catherine of Aragon's plea to King Henry VIII while the director flipped through a pile of paper. But I also spoke about my positive experiences, preparation, etiquette, proper dress, and call-backs. Rejection was a painful part of the process. This could have nothing to do with a person's talent! The director often is casting a certain look in actors. Will they make a good picture on stage? In the acting world, as the saying went, you had to pick yourself up, brush yourself off and start all over again. Like life itself.

I heard the drums as I walked on the sidewalk in front of Carlisle Gym. I could not wait. I felt such a release in African Dance moving to the pounding rhythms of the twelve shirtless, buff musicians. I forgot everything and just experienced joy. Toward the end of class we formed into straight lines that took turns dancing in front of the drummers. My body responded freely to the smiling, laughing drummers who looked us straight in the eye. My heart filled with passion for life. I felt strong and confident. For the moment.

Murder at Theatre X

I gulped water from my bottle on the way out the door still wearing my animal print ethnic skirt, black leotard, and shell anklet. Questions and worries flooded back in my mind. Olive! And the rest of her possibly murderous relatives! Did one of them try to shoot James and killed his first wife? Did her sister Marnie murder her estranged professor husband? I already knew what Olive could do! What a gene pool.

The fresh air cooled my hot, red face. I saw Jane Keyes and Isabel the Flamenco dancer sitting on the low circular concrete wall bordering an elevated lush lawn in front of Carlisle Gym. Should I join them or pass by? I stopped. Paralyzed ambivalence again! Enough of that!

"Hi!" I said and perched up on the rim. Isabel burst into tears and threw her arms around me.

Christina Squire

Chapter 54

"Isabel! Isabel! What happened?" I asked as she sobbed into my sweaty neck. I patted her back. I saw Jane shaking her head.

"I didn't know!" Isabel screamed. "I didn't know!"

"Didn't know what, Isabel?"

"*No sabia...*" she sobbed.

Vincente and Joaquin burst out of the gym. Isabel jumped down from the rim and ran to them. They embraced her and spoke softly in Spanish. I looked at Jane. She shook her head again. Vincente was holding a limp Isabel and whispering in her ear. She was choking and moaning. He slowly walked away with her clinging to him. Joaquin turned toward us.

"Leave Isabel alone!" he said. He gritted his white teeth. "You upset her again, and you'll be sorry!" He pointed at Jane. "*Vete a la mierda policia!*" Then he looked at me, spit on the ground and hissed. "*Puta!*" He ran to catch up with Isabel and Vincente.

Jane and I sat silently. "Charming guy," I finally said.

"I think he told me to fuck myself," she said.

"Well, I'm a whore."

175

"They care about Isa—" Jane said and then burst out laughing. "Caro! I'm trying to be serious!"

"Go on!"

"There is a video, Caro."

"Let me guess...Professor Smith was involved."

"Somehow he edited the video she sent in with her application for an MFA in Dance. In the original Isabel is dancing the *Sevillanas* outdoors with a group of young people. Now the film has several couples starting to dance but gradually begin to take off their festive clothes and have sex: on the ground, under trees and bushes: And keeping time with the music with their contortions, thrusting, and sucking. A travesty. Cuts of Isabel dancing and smiling are woven between shots of pornography. This gives the impression that she is celebrating the orgy. And her name is the first one listed in the credits!"

"Awful. I am so sorry. She didn't report him?"

"Blackmail. Her mother, brothers and sisters are living in poverty in Mexico. And Richard threatened her with expulsion from the graduate program. She needs this degree to get a good paying job at a prestigious dance academy in Mexico City."

"Did the video go viral? Did Richard post it on a site?"

"Well, some guy saw it and told Vincente. He was shocked and mad. But Vincente told Isabel that he could not find it anywhere."

"When did this happen?"

"The week before school started."

"That's why she was screaming at him when I went to his office."

Murder at Theatre X

"I remember you told us about that."

"Isabel was hysterical! She told me his was the devil… how did you find out about the video?"

Jane hopped off the concrete ledge. "Can you come to my office?"

"Not now. I have another class. I have to change clothes."

"I'll walk you back to the department."

Christina Squire

Chapter 55

"I wanted to ask Isabel about Marnie. Was Olive always with her sister? Did she ever hear them talking…" Jane said as we passed the Geology Building and turned left to walk up the narrow mall past the Art and Art History Building. "She said Olive was always there, but she never heard them talking. Then I asked her about her video. She freaked out on me, gestured wildly and said something in Spanish. She walked away from me!"

"You were asking about her graduate project film, weren't you?"

"Of course! Trying to make conversation. To engage."

We slowly walked up the wide steep steps at the back of the Fine Arts Center. My calf muscles were twitching from flinging myself around. "So what did you do?"

"Well, I caught up with her. I said that I wanted to see her film. She screamed 'No you don't'. I asked her to please talk to me. And she did. Horrible."

"Oh yes..," I said. "Jane! We have to find that video! Maybe Richard has it on his phone? Do you have his phone?"

"His phone is missing. And his keys."

"We have to see that video," I said.

"I'll go back to my office to see if I can find it on line," she said.

"I know someone close by who has a 27-inch IMac and loves intrigue." We went to the Theatre Office.

"Clarence!" I said loudly. He kept typing.

"We need you!" I said loudly. He kept typing.

Jane leaned over the desk and stuck her badge in front of his face. "I don't have time for this."

"Well!" He slowly turned around. "If it isn't Wonder Woman and Miss Marple. Together at last. How do I rate this honor?"

"We need to search for a video that Professor Smith made. He may have posted it on line before he was murdered," Jane said.

Clarence opened a drawer, pulled out scissors and a bag of Baked Lays Potato Chips, snipped it open and took one chip daintily out. He bit off half of it with his beautiful white teeth and chewed like he had all the time in the world. Clarence even made baked chips look good.

"So easy!" he said. "Anyone can do it!" He wiped his hands with Wet Ones.

"So please let me use your computer," Jane said.

"Oh please let me," he said holding his hands in prayer. "But there must be a hard copy of the video somewhere. I told Inspector Hutchinson that the UPS package that came for Professor Smith was from Vimeo."

"But where is it?" I asked.

"We looked at all his belongings: office and house—" Jane said.

"---Did you look in his briefcase?" I interrupted her. They both looked at me like I was an idiot. "False bottoms! I watched a Miss Fisher mystery where the murderer hid an incriminating document in the false bottom of his suitcase!"

"A good suggestion, Caro," Jane sighed. "A common mystery trope."

Clarence looked at his nails. "Yes, quite a trope, Caro."

I ignored him. An idea was forming in my head. "Has anyone checked the department DVD players?" I asked. "My husband thought I threw away his Jack Halloran Christmas carol tape. I always hated their twee sound but denied getting rid of it."

Clarence rudely turned away and started typing.

"John looked through his tape collection—" I went on.

"Tape collection?" Clarence snarked. He folded up the baked chips, stuck a large paper clip on top and replaced them in a drawer. He sashayed around his desk.

"Yes," I said. "He still has music tapes! He doesn't listen to them anymore, but they're lined up on his closet shelf. Anyway, I got sick of all the drama and finally looked in our dusty tape deck in the den closet. There it was. Not played since the last Christmas."

Clarence moved his hand in a circle. "And?"

"...So our family joke, when we used to joke, was whenever something was missing we said, 'Look in the tape deck.'" I laughed. They stared at me. Seriously speechless. "So let's look in the DVD players!"

"Come on!" Clarence said.

181

"Lead on, Macduff!" I said.

"Actually, Caro," Jane said, "the quote from the Scottish Play is Lay on, Macduff."

"Snap!"

"I majored in English," she added.

"Lead! Lay! *Andele!*" Clarence locked the office door behind us.

"I bet Richard tossed the Vimeo packaging in a recycle bin," I said as we went down the stairs.

"More dumpster diving, Caro?" Jane asked.

"You know I love it!"

Chapter 56

"Wait!" I said. "I have to change clothes in Sam's office! I have a class in 30 minutes!" Jane checked her phone. Clarence leaned against the lockers and shook his head.

I tore off my dance outfit, unhooked my shell ankle bracelet, stepped into my jeans, sketchers, and put the John Lennon tee over my head. I shot out of the office.

"Finally!" Clarence said.

"What if the Professor played the DVD on his computer?" I said. "And we're just wasting time!"

"He didn't," Jane said. "He had a new IMac. Can't play DVDs on them. Most people stream movies now. But one can get a special USB cord to hook up a DVD player to your computer anyway."

"Huh."

Jane and I followed Clarence down a dark narrow hall under the stairs. He unlocked the door with his master key. I wished I had one! He turned on the light in the closet. There were shelves of old VCR tape players, wires and extension cords. Clarence rolled two

183

carts of TVs the size of washing machines out in the hall. "I don't know why we still have to keep this junk!" he bitched.

We saw three BluRay players on the back shelf alongside three 27 inch flat screen TVs.

"We shall see what we shall see," Jane said. She took latex gloves out of her cross-body bag. How prepared is that, I thought enviously. She pushed the eject buttons on the DVD players. Empty...empty...a disc. She carefully lifted it out. Jane read the label out loud: "*Sevillanas Sabrosas*". With her other hand, she pulled her cell phone out of her pocket, and punched one number. "James. Get over to the theatre basement now...yes...yes."

"Oh goody," Clarence said.

"Have to go to class," I called as I walked away.

"Thank you, Caro," Jane said.

I had a brief snit. Once again my ideas helped those two. And now I cannot watch the DVD! But Jane did thank me. Something! Could they wait for me? Of course not. I could skip class. But I really did not want to see James. I had a shame storm thinking that I said the wrong thing when I quoted from the book.... He was so upset...shaken. Me and my big mouth.

But too bad!

I had to perform a scene from *The Bald Soprano* in a few minutes. I went over my lines outside the classroom. They were so absurd that my character the Maid could probably recite the Miranda Rights and fit right in.

I had a rehearsal tonight for *Act Without Words II* with the goad. Max better get his butt down here to operate it and bring me a Frontier Fiesta burger. I'll text him.

What was on that disc, I wondered. Poor Isabel.

Christina Squire

Chapter 57

I finally checked out a locker. About time. Poor Sam's office could not hold another one of my possessions. I stuffed my dance clothes, text books and notebooks in there. I moved a bag of props, the goad and coffee sacks for the Beckett play to an empty classroom I had reserved for rehearsal. I moved the desks against the wall. I had 30 minutes before my actors came. And where was Max? The little darling! I was punching in a pithy text message when my Inspector walked in.

"Hi!" I said.

"I'm here to help, Caro." James handed me a white bag on his way to the goad. He picked it up. "Max can't make it tonight."

"Really, now!" I took out a hamburger and drink.

"He has an emergency acolyte meeting at the church." James spinned the wheels.

"Oh those acolytes! Probably planning a mutiny!" He didn't laugh. Uh oh. I unwrapped the burger. "Thank you, James."

"Max told me."

James got down on the floor. He set the goad on its wheels. I sat next to him.

"The goad comes out stage left behind a curtain," I said. "I'll tape the floor here to show where the curtain will be. The goad will roll out showing one wheel to dart the first sack and show both wheels to dart the second sack."

"I've read the play, Caro." He slowly rolled the pointed head back and forth.

"Of course you have." Silly me. I watched the goad go back and forth. Back and forth. I took huge bites of the burger.

"Am I doing this right?" he asked.

"Oh yeah." (I'll say, I thought!) I could not watch anymore! I stood up, wiped my chin with a napkin and tossed the wrapper in a wastebasket. "Did Jane show you the---?"

"Hello Caro!" Bill and Alan came in. "Are we on time?"

"Yes! Hi! OK! I have props! This is James who is going to operate the goad tonight. James, my actors, Bill and Alan."

They greeted each other. The guys took off their jeans. They were wearing extra large button-up shirts that hung mid thigh on them. I gave Alan who was playing the morose bagman a bottle of pills to put in his shirt pocket. I gave Bill, the perky bagman, a watch, comb, and toothbrush to put in his pocket. I filled the pockets of a coat with a carrot, a mirror, a map, a compass, and a clothes brush. I neatly folded the coat and a pair of pants on the floor between the bags and placed a pair of boots and a hat on top of the clothes.

The rehearsal went well except for Alan and Bill giggling inside their sacks. They shrieked the first few times the goad poked them when it was time to emerge. Even James cracked a smile. This was not Beckett's intention! I had to use my Mom voice (not that any of my children ever paid attention). We were going up in one week! We had to get serious! Thankfully, the guys pantomimed their moods well and smoothly used their props. I was so relieved to see that they moved well.

I could use Theatre X to rehearse two days before the performance. I was able to store the bags, clothes, goad and props in its prop room that was finally opened after the forensic team investigation. We set a rehearsal time for the next week. I'll ask my sister to do the lights. I needed one bright light coming from stage right. She was technical. She'll figure it out.

Christina Squire

Chapter 58

James silently helped me gather up the props and move the chairs back to the middle of the classroom. I was so worried that he was upset with me. It was always about me. I had to let that go. For now.

"Did you watch the video?" I asked.

"Yes." James stuffed boots, pants and hat into one coffee sack. "It was awful." He tossed the sack near the door and got the goad. "I had just finished it when Max texted me to ask if I could pick up food and go to your rehearsal. The video was very hard to watch. I was upset and mad as hell. I thought about my daughter Claire. Isabel. I thought about the young girls in the film. Where did they come from? Where are they now? Awful."

"Horrible," I said as I put the rest of the props in the overcoat's large pockets and packed it all in the other sack.

"But we could not find that film anywhere on the internet. And Clarence knew sites I'd never heard of. So maybe the good professor took it down before he was murdered. Or was forced to. It may still be on his

191

phone, wherever that is. But we have the disc thanks to you, Caro. Jane told me." James picked up both sacks. I got the goad. I turned off the light.

"You're welcome, James."

We walked down the hall. It was empty except for one student sitting against a wall studying a script. She smiled at James. Well, who wouldn't?

"I've issued a search warrant for Joaquin and Vincente's apartment," he said.

"What?"

"We're looking for a knife. Maybe a phone. They have motivation."

"True."

"Professor Smith was decapitated after he was poisoned. There was not a lot of blood in the sacks with his body or head or anywhere else."

"Someone else could have poisoned him?"

James shrugged. "Maybe."

I unlocked Theatre X. I had a key for it since I was directing a play in that space. The ghost light cast an eerie shadow on the black box stage. "Olive was on opioids for her broken wrist! She claimed they caused her to confess to murder! Fentanyl?" I said.

"Jane is checking Olive's medical records."

"Joaquin and Vincente love Isabel---so...They would take revenge. But why cut off his head if he's already dead?" I unlocked the prop room door and held it open for James.

"A message? Satisfaction? Pure anger? Let's not try to know." James hauled the bags in.

OK. I won't, I thought. Now time for me. I flipped on the light. What a sight! People! Get it together, I thought! Props of all shapes and sizes seemed to have been shoveled back into this room after the police evidence crew were done sweeping it for clues. What a bunch of junk. I put down the goad and started moving objects out of the way to make room for my junk. And I took a deep breath. "James, I may have misspoken about the Chinese saying and given you false hope and upset—"

"Caro! Please! There is definitely a coincidence. And maybe a story!" He was lifting a huge vase of fake flowers upright so he could prop the goad up against the wall. "My contacts in New Orleans are checking if Captain Maupassant is related to Olive. You and Max helped me." He neatly stacked cups next to the teapot. "She is too familiar with my life in New Orleans for her not to be getting information from someone."

I collected loose spoons, forks, and chopsticks to put them next to plates and empty Chinese take out cartons. I stopped suddenly and looked at James. Really looked at him. Without frantic desire. This man who was picking up artificial fruit. Who experienced grief, guilt, and injustice. This married man whose wife was asleep half way across the world. And who was dedicated to solving the murder of his beloved first wife.

A man with issues.

A man I thought I loved. And yet...did we have a story?

Christina Squire

Chapter 59

"Do we have a story?" I asked.

"What?" James turned around holding a bunch of wax grapes.

"I was wondering if—"

"What are you holding?" He put the grapes next to a dial phone.

"What? Oh…spoons, forks, chopsticks…." I held them like a bouquet.

"Let me see the chopsticks."

"OK…here…" I watched James lift out nine chopsticks. All were solid black plastic except for one decorated with a cloisonné flower. "Oh no!" I shrieked.

"Yes!" James said.

"No! Not again! Is it Olive's?"

"We'll find out!"

With one hand James pulled a pair of latex gloves and a plastic bag out of his pocket. I marveled at how prepared police were at all times. Or at least the two I knew. I wanted to be prepared!

195

He was all business. "Hold this."

I held the cloisonné chopstick by its sharp end. I felt a chill flashing back once again to the time Olive jabbed a chopstick in front of my face. James pulled on the gloves, took it away from me and put it in a plastic bag. He snapped his gloves off.

"Good work, Caro."

"Well, damn! Olive is going to think we planted another piece of incriminating evidence against her!"

"I'll have to work hard and fast to collect more evidence. I can and I will!"

"I will, too! And Jane! But how did Olive get in here? Did she have the professor's keys? They have been missing,"

He looked dazed like he just woke up out of a trance. "Of course…someone has them…yes…what did you ask me?"

"Oh that…I was thinking about coincidence and stories."

"And?" He moved close to me.

I had to think fast. I cleared my throat. "And I'm wondering about the coincidence that last year we found one of Olive's possessions that incriminated her and now may have found another."

"Now there's a story!" James said.

"Huh."

We heard a knock. "James! Are you in there?" I opened the door. I saw the woman who was sitting in the hall: pretty, petite, dark hair in a pony tail, wearing tattered jeans, black converse tennis shoes, and a La Chat Lunatique tee.

"And you are?" I asked.

"She's Maggie the Private Eye, Caro," James said.

Of course, I remembered. James hired her to follow Olive. And she was Jane's partner.

"Olive is in the building," Maggie said. "She's in Professor Richard's office. First she tried to get into Theatre X."

"She has keys!" I said.

James pushed by both of us. "She's got some explaining to do—"

Maggie grabbed his arm. "James! Wait! Don't confront her now! I called the UNM Police. They're contacting Jane! Calm down!"

"I know what I'm doing!" He yanked his arm out of her grasp and walked away.

I ran in front of him and put both hands on his chest. "James! Listen to Maggie! Do not see Olive in this condition. Nothing gives her more joy than upsetting you! Breathe!" He walked around me but collapsed in a theatre seat.

"For a while Olive stood outside the classroom when you had rehearsal, Caro," Maggie said.

"Great." My stomach turned over.

"She and her wretched relatives are going down! A nest of vipers!" James said.

Maggie sat beside him. "In time, in time."

Lieutenant Jane Keyes rushed in. "Olive's sister Marnie just picked her up by the loading dock."

"I have to talk to you, Jane," he said.

Christina Squire

***

The three of them formed a tight little group. Well!
Dis me, butts! So what! I'd had a long day. I suddenly
felt so tired and ready to burst into tears. I said my
goodbyes, as if they cared, went home, passed by my
sons' closed doors, rushed in the bathroom and threw
up the Fiesta Burger.

Chapter 60

"You did what?" my sister Sally yelled. We were driving down Central to the university.

"I told the chair you were doing the lights for—"

"No, Caro! Not that! You told me that you threw up last night! You haven't thrown up for 35 years! I remember you crying and choking and mother holding your head."

"I hate to throw up. I can't seem to get the hang of it. Stuff goes up my nose and—"

"You never even had morning sickness with three pregnancies!"

I had already calmed myself down by remembering that last night. I absolutely could not be pregnant. Had to be a bad Frontier burger. Then I thought Olive made me sick.

"I have a 24 hour flu." My Cheerios breakfast was not agreeing with me. I took a swig of Sprite. Sally was making me nervous. "I've been working very hard—"

"Have you been using protection?"

I got hot all over and swerved my Beetle into the parking space behind the Fine Arts Center. Actually using birth control never crossed my mind. John had had a vasectomy 15 years ago. I was not used to thinking about it. Stupid. Out of control. Thank God. But I said, "Whatever do you mean?" I knew exactly what she meant.

"You know damn well what I mean." She got out of the car and slammed the door.

"I am old, Sally, and it's not like we've been together that way…a lot—"

"You're not that old! What? 45? And it only takes once!"

"Can't a woman vomit without people jumping to conclusions? I just wanted a little sympathy from you!" I said. "And I want you to check out these lights!" I stomped into the building. My sister was so intense. I knew she cared, a lot, but she was so protective of me and my family. She thought she had to advise us on all matters as if we were challenged. Well…I may be in a challenging condition…and need her…Was that really why I told her?

"And James could have a disease!" she called out. "Why didn't you tell him to wear a condom?"

"For God's sake lower your voice!"

We rummaged around behind the second layer of heavy black curtains on each side of the Theatre X stage. Black cylinder lights lay on the floor against the back wall.

Murder at Theatre X

"You will use just one," I said. "Just a strong single beam coming from stage right, Beckett said."

Sally picked one up by its handle and plugged it in. "No problem." A bright stream of light shot across the stage. "Snap!"

"Sally! That's just what I want!" I said. "Thank you!"

"Why are you using that light?" John walked into Theatre X with Max.

He looked tall and handsome, as usual, but I got a headache in my eye. "What are you doing here?"

"Max said you were designing the lighting for your play today. I used to do lights for Highland High School productions. Thought I could be of some use."

"I asked Sally. She figured it out."

"I did, John," said Sally.

He threw up his hands. "Ok. I'm not needed."

Poor him.

"Right. You're not needed," I said. I turned to Max. "And why are you out of school?"

"I am in DECA. I'm doing a project with Dad's accounting firm."

"Distributive Education Clubs of America? *BUSINESS?*"

"What's wrong with business?" John asked.

"I'm going into management," Max said.

"Of course you are," I said. Max had managed me all his life.

"Why are you so pale?" Max asked.

"I have the flu."

"Go home, Mom." He put his arm around me. I almost burst into tears. What's with these emotions?

201

"I think I will, honey—"

"I need to talk to you," John said.

"I don't feel good," I said.

"Just a few minutes, Caro."

"Dad! Mom doesn't feel good!" Max said.

John ignored him. "Please."

"Let's go out on the loading dock," I sighed. Max frowned.

"Come see what these lights can do, Max," Sally said.

Max sat down beside her.

Chapter 61

We stood on the loading dock. John lit a cigarette. Bile rose up in my throat. I waved the smoke away.

"Sorry," John said and blew a stream of smoke away from me. "You quit?"

"I'm sick."

He put it out then loomed over me. I stepped away. He started toward me again. I stopped him with a look. He spread his hands. "I miss you, Caro."

Silence.

"I love you."

Silence.

"I want to come back home."

"Then I'm moving out," I said.

"To play house with that inspector?"

"No!"

"Whatever you say... I am very disappointed in you, Caro. So is my mother. And does your father know what you're doing?"

"Your mother has always been disappointed in me, and my father just wants me to be happy." Actually, my father's first priority was his wife, my stepmother.

203

I believed he loved my sister and me but left us quite alone. He called once a week to see how I was, but we just talked about the boys and his bridge tournaments.

"The family is the foundation of society, and—," John intoned.

"Oh shut up, John!"

"You don't understand my vulnerability! I am so unhappy! I'm lost without you! I can't concentrate at work! I turned to Alice out of desperation and loneliness. You and I have reached out to others for comfort—"

"Reaching out, is it? What a turn of phrase," I said.

"Listen to me! I am willing to forgive and forget—"

"Spare me your willingness to sacrifice and holier than thou pronouncements! I don't care what you think!"

"You don't care."

"I don't care." I turned to walk into the building. But I did care. I felt smothered by his presence and had to lash out. Was it guilt? That I committed adultery? That I may be carrying another man's child? John was being sincere. But he wore me out. He sucked all the energy out of me. I was weak. What have I done? I could not deal with him now. I had to leave quickly.

John grabbed my arm stopping me mid-flight. "You will never find anyone who loves you as much as I do."

That did it. My doubts flew. I yanked my arm away. "No shit?"

Hot, angry tears ran down my face. He may be right. But did I want that kind of love?

John opened his arms to hug me. "Oh Caro," he said.

I stepped back.

John shook his head, walked to the Fine Arts Center doors, and passed James who was coming out. "Don't hurt her," he said and went inside.

"What happened?" James asked.

"I have to throw up." I ran inside and down the steps to the women's dressing room. I just made it to the toilet. James held my head and rubbed my back. I cried in between hurling Cheerios and Sprite. When I was finished James splashed water on my face and dried it with his hankie. He half-carried my limp body to a chair.

"Did John make you sick?" he asked with a grin.

"Yes! And Olive made me sick last night!"

"A capital offense! I will bring charges!" James lifted me out of the chair, sat down and pulled me onto his lap. I laid my head on his chest and inhaled his clean scent. I was mentally, physically, and emotionally exhausted. I fell asleep.

Christina Squire

Chapter 62

"There you are!"

Sally's loud voice woke me up. I blinked. James was reading something on his cell phone. I could not move. I did not want to move.

James turned off his phone. I lifted my head. He still held me close.

"I have been looking all over this rat's maze of a building for you, Caro," she yelled. "I thought something horrible happened! And I find you asleep in the arms of…of…"

"James," James said.

"James…Right…You scared me to death, Caro! All the murders on this campus! And I am missing my Tai Chi class! I'm glad you're getting a nap! Must be nice!"

I sat up. "Do you have any gum? Or a mint?" Ugh. My breath.

"You left me to deal with your distraught husband and my worried nephew—" Sally dug through her huge bucket bag, took out a stick of ginseng gum, unwrapped it, and gave it to me. "And then I walked up and down these halls knocking on classroom doors—"

207

"She was sick, Sally," James said.

"I know. She threw up last night," she said. "She told me she had the flu, but I wonder if she's not—"

"Sally! Please!" I shouted.

"She's not what?" James asked.

"There you are!" Jane Keyes walked in and saw James. She took in the dressing room tableau. "I heard all this screaming."

I stood up. "My sister and I were just talking the Macedonian way. Jane, this is Sally. Sally, meet Lieutenant Keyes of the UNM police department."

They shook hands. James got up and gently sat me down.

"What's going on?" Jane asked.

"I have the flu."

"I'm sorry, Caro," she said then turned to James. "We searched Vincente and Joaquin's house and Isabelle's apartment and found nothing incriminating. We are testing all the kitchen knives, though, but none look big or sharp enough to be able to decapitate a person. No opiods."

"Thank you," James said. "I want to confirm Marnie and Olive's alibis for the day and night of the professor's murder. They said they went to the movie with their mother. And we need fingerprint results on the chopstick."

"They're Olive's," Jane said.

"Oh she'll have some excuse!" I said. "Like she was in the Theatre X prop room looking for a lamp for Marnie or a table for Isabelle, or something!"

"But CSI didn't clear the prop room until yesterday," Jane said. "Olive can't make that excuse!"

Murder at Theatre X

"That's why she was prowling around Theatre X last night! She wanted to get in the Prop Room! But we were in there!" I cried.

"I'm driving my sister home. She does not need to get more agitated," Sally said.

"Of course," James said. He took my hands and raised me up. "I'll walk her to the car."

"I feel like an idiot," I said.

When we got home I brushed my teeth and took a hot bath. I put on a pair of soft men's boxer shorts and tissue tee. Max and Douglas made me cups of tea and cinnamon toast. I had a small bowl of happy chicken and rice soup Douglas had bought at Sprout's. My sister quietly stayed until I went to bed.

I did not throw up.

Thank God.

Christina Squire

Chapter 63

But I did the next morning. I was getting kind of good at it.

Must have the 48 hour flu. But no fever. No body aches. Hmmm.

Yeah...hmmm all right. I could not think about the other possibility now. My show was going up this weekend. Rehearsal tonight in Theatre X. I had a paper due on performance theory: All the world's a stage. I'll write about Olive. How murderers act their way out of a confession. Write what you know.

Max left for school before I got up. I could only hope. James called. I lied and told him I felt better. And no, thank you, I didn't need anything. But I tear up at the sound of his voice. Sally called. Yes, I threw up again. And no, I will not talk about it! I had to hold the phone away from my ear.

Douglas brought me a cup of tea, cinnamon toast, and sliced raw apple before he went to his first university class. "Mom! I made a thermos full of tea for you."

"Thank you, honey," I said as I crawled back into bed with my laptop.

"I wish you could stay home," he said.

"I'll just go in, make some copies for Theatre Appreciation, skip African Dance, and take a nap before rehearsal."

He leaned over and hugged me. "I love you, Douglas."

"Text me if you need anything."

"I'll be fine. I'm just overdone." I could only hope.

"Your butt's getting bigger."

I was bending over picking up Sam's book on Beckett's short plays that was on the bottom shelf of the mail slots.

I turned around. Clarence sat at his desk reaching into his lunch bag.

"Thank you ever so, Clarence! You always make me feel good."

"I try, girlfriend!" He unwrapped a peanut butter and jelly bagel and took a huge bite.

I collapsed in the chair in front of his desk. "Now I have the flu and a big butt."

He rolled his chair back against the wall. "The flu! Don't come near me! You should not be here! Go home!"

Louise opened her door. She looked me up and down.

"Hi, Louise," I said.

No response. What else was new?

"Do you have those reports ready for the Dean, Clarence? I meet with him in an hour."

Murder at Theatre X

"In your box."

"Thanks." She took the forms out of her mailbox on top of a file cabinet, went in her office and slammed the door.

"I don't understand why she hates me so much." I stood up.

Clarence put down his bagel, swanned around his desk, and motioned me to go out in the hall. "Oh Caro! It's not about you!" he whispered. "Her husband is dying. She's keeping him at home with hospice care."

"I'm sorry. I did not know. Cancer?"

"Yes."

"I—"

"You woulda thought!" Brianne wobbled up to us on black patent leather high heels wearing a black sheath dress, black fishnet hose, a strand of black pearls and a wisp of black netting covered her bright red fox bangs.

"Coulda, woulda, shoulda what, Brianne?" Clarence sneered.

"You WOULD HAVE thought the department WOULD HAVE closed for Richard's memorial service!" She yelled.

Louise stuck her head out the door. "My decision."

"You cunt!" Brianne hissed.

"Go to Hell, Brianne," Louise slammed her door. Again. Brianne turned and left.

Silence.

"Those black pearls cost a lot," I finally said.

"So does she...Let's sit on the bench outside Rodey Theatre. You look pale."

213

Christina Squire

Chapter 64

"So what's wrong with you?" Clarence asked before taking another bite of his bagel. He had brought his sack lunch and closed the office for the noon hour.

"I'm tired and weepy and nauseated," I said.

"Hmmm. Are you still seeing that delicious Inspector?"

"Off and on…" I took the thermos out of my purse and poured a cup of tea.

"And hubby?" Clarence peeled a banana.

"Moved out."

"Girl! All this and graduate school! Why are you torturing yourself? Take a leave of absence before you collapse! I care!"

I laughed. "Well, that makes one person in the main office! But I think Louise dislikes Brianne more than me!"

"Stop having a pity party with yourself! You are too sensitive! I told you that Louise has a lot on her mind. And dislike is not the word I would use to describe how she feels about Brianne."

"Why?"

Clarence finished the banana and opened a small bag of baby carrots. "Because Brianne broke up Louise's 30 year marriage."

"What?"

"And Professor Smith introduced Brianne to Frank, let them use his cabin in Chama for weekend trysts, and taunted Louise about her husband. He knew intimate facts about their marriage that Frank had told Brianne in moments of passion. Information she was only too delighted to share with Richard."

"When was this?"

"Two years ago. Louise was elected chair. Then... well...Men can be pigs." He crunched carrots and offered me one.

"No thanks...but Louise is living with her husband now."

I saw Douglas walking across the foyer to us. He handed me a carton of yogurt and plastic spoon. "Mom! I bought you a little something at the Coop branch in the Bookstore. Might settle your stomach."

"Thank you, honey! Douglas this is Clarence."

Clarence stood up all animated. "Nice to meet you."

"Can you join us?"

"No. Have to go to Percussion Ensemble down in the basement."

"Well! He is handsome!" Clarence said as he watched Douglas walk away.

"Thank you. And he's nice. And a talented musician."

"Any of your sons gay?"

"I don't think so."

"Damn."

"Oh Clarence! You're too much!" I tasted a bit of strawberry yogurt. So good! Suddenly I was starving. "Now where were we? Louise is caring for her husband at home..."

"Brianne dumped him when he got sick. Louise got word they were not together anymore but not why. When Louise went to their family doctor for a check-up, he told her how sorry he was about Frank's pancreatic cancer. She didn't know! She didn't even know where he lived!"

"I will have some carrots," I said.

"Louise looked up Brianne's schedule of classes. She barged into a Film Noir seminar that Richard was teaching. Richard laughed and told the class to excuse the bad manners of one of his returning students. But Brianne did give Louise the address."

"Awful!"

"Louise had to practically scrape Frank up off the floor of his studio apartment and brought him home."

I licked the yogurt lid. "Do you have any baked chips?"

"In my desk."

"Oh. Well...go on!"

"Louise shared the full catastrophe with me over coffee. She wanted to explain why she was so distracted and asked me to please have patience with her as she assumed responsibilities as chair. And she needed my help getting to know the office routines. She did not plan to have the chairmanship and her husband's adultery dumped in her lap at the same time."

"And then Brianne took up with the good professor."

"She was already fucking him, I'm sure!" Clarence drained a full bottle of water.

"Why was Professor Smith so hateful to Louise?"

"She didn't give him what he wanted. His plan was to merge the Cinematic Arts and Theatre Departments and head them both. He then could control the curriculum, the plays offered, and all the creative writing programs…He wanted to drive her crazy…and honestly, Caro, I think he succeeded."

Chapter 65

I made a hard copy of *Footfalls* then set the Xerox machine to make 150 stapled copies. Clarence called out to me.

"Can you answer the phones while I go to the bathroom? I don't want to close the office."

"Of course." I sat down at his pristine desk. I was still hungry and craved baked potato chips. I opened drawers until I found the bag, neatly folded up and secured with a large paper clip. Must not get stale! I took the bag out. Underneath was an opened box of Periwinkle Super Stretch Nitrile gloves. Don't mind if I do, I thought, as I took out two gloves. I wanted to be prepared, too, like my Inspector and Jane Keyes. Ready in a flash to handle any evidence!

"What are you doing?" Clarence walked in.

"I wanted some baked chips but found these gloves. I took two. Hope you don't mind." I rose up out of his throne.

"For fun and games with your inspector?"

"No, Clarence! I want to be prepared in case I find any evidence!"

219

"Of course you do." Clarence waltzed back around his desk. "I use those when I clean out lockers at the end of each semester...a gross job if you recall."

I remembered when Clarence opened all the lockers in the men's dressing room when we were looking for evidence related to the Art Museum murder over a year ago.

Homeless men showered and stored their few possessions in there. Just the memory of smelling dirty underwear, rotten food, and broken bottles of liquor made me lose my appetite. I put the chips back in the drawer.

The phone rang. "Yes, yes, I will. Don't worry. I'll bring it right over." Clarence said and hung up. "Great! Louise is meeting with the Dean. She needs the enrollment stats for the last five years!" He started working on his computer. "Crap! I downloaded the information on a thumb drive so she could work on it at home and then dumped the original in a folder! I can't find it!"

The phone rang. "Can you hold?" he said and turned to me. "Caro! Check Louise's desk for the drive! I have to talk to the *Journal* Venue editor about our current productions so they can print it Friday! We need a PR person! I can't do everything!"

I entered her inner sanctum. Healthy plants were on file cabinets. Posters of past university plays, a diploma from Tisch School of the Arts, a framed newspaper article praising her direction of *The Collection* hung on the walls. Classical music played softly on an aqua retro clock radio. I scanned the top of her desk. There was only a photograph of a younger, smiling Louise and a slight, bearded man sitting under an umbrella on a beach. Must be poor Frank. I opened drawers: notebooks, hanging files, folders, pens, post-it notes, hand lotion and a large bottle of Advil. The lowest, deep drawer had socks, a small umbrella, a knit hat, and two periwinkle Nitrile gloves.

My heart started pounding. I heard Clarence listing the upcoming plays. Then he hung up.

"Not here!" I called.

What should I do? I got hot all over. My head was spinning. This could be nothing! My imagination ran wild. Louise probably had access to fentanyl for her husband's pain. And wore gloves to smear it on Richard?

Oh no. I needed to throw up.

"Never mind!" Clarence yelled. "I found it! She gave the thumb drive back to me after all. My brain is fried working here! I have to do every damn thing!"

I slipped on the pair of gloves I got out of Clarence's drawer, picked up one glove, and put it in my tunic pocket.

I came out and closed the door.

"Your copying is done, girlfriend."

"I'll be right back." I ran.

Christina Squire

Chapter 66

I took a mind deadening nap with my dog that afternoon. I woke up and thought about John. Was this the end of our marriage? I could not bear to be around his all consuming, energy sucking presence anymore. I felt quite good without him. My pregnancy will certainly end our future together. And change my own future. Open some doors? One should say yes to new life, shouldn't one? I wanted to say yes to my life, though. Oh I will say yes to life! Period!

I missed my mother.

What if James did not love me? "I will survive," I said. This woke Suki up. She laid her head on my stomach. I kissed her and pet her. Now her love I needed every minute of the day.

I had to get ready for rehearsal tonight. I had things to do besides thinking about who loved me or not! I made myself a cup of tea and peanut butter toast. I left money on the kitchen counter for Max and Douglas to buy dinner. I could not remember the last time I cooked a meal. I was getting fat from eating carry out or perhaps for some other reason. I texted Max about rehearsal tonight just in case he forgot, the little darling.

My bag guys Alan and Bill were sitting on the floor outside Theatre X. My sister and Max weren't here yet, but I was early. They asked if they could get coffee at the SUB. I said OK. I unlocked the doors, turned on the light, and headed to the prop room. I opened the door. The house lights in the Theatre lit up the Prop Room, too. Suddenly there was a shadow, and I smelled a heady mixture of Joy perfume and cigarettes. I whipped around. There was Olive. Close to me. So close to me. Made me nauseated. Maybe I'll throw up on her and ruin one of her silk jumpsuits. Her long platinum hair hung in snaky strands around her shoulders. Her face heavily made up. Her violet lipstick bled into the cracks around her mouth. The thick black kohl lining brought out the red streaks in the whites of her eyes.

"Hello, Olive," I said like greeting an old friend. I was terrified but determined not to show it. My knees shook. I got light-headed. I casually leaned against a shelf. 'What are doing here?" As if I didn't know! Where in the hell was Maggie who was supposed to be following her?

"Cut the act, you little tramp. Get out of my way!" She pushed me aside. She scanned the props and found the jar holding the chopsticks. Olive took them all, pushed me again with such force that I fell down, and walked out.

Murder at Theatre X

"I especially liked the cloisonné one!" I yelled on my hands and knees.

She turned around. I crawled to the goad.

But Max beat her through the door and picked up the goad. "I'm here to help," he said holding the goad straight in front of him.

"You and yours will be very, very sorry," Olive whispered. And disappeared.

"Mom! Are you all right?" Max held my hands and lifted me up off the floor.

"Now I am! Thank you, honey!"

Alan, Bill, and Sally gathered around the Prop Room.

I took a deep breath. "Let's start," I said and walked with quivering legs onto the stage. The show must go on!

Christina Squire

Chapter 67

Rehearsal went well. Max had to practice timing with the goad. Sally just flipped on the harsh light beam, and that was that. I sat in the audience and admired the way the young men pantomimed their actions. I laughed at their expressions: one so morose and one so happy doing the same things! They were good. I hoped their acting teacher came to the show.

My heart beat normally again. After rehearsal was over I had to contact Jane and my Inspector. Not only for my sake but for my loved ones' safety. How dare Olive include my children in her psychotic plans for revenge! Chilled me.

Olive must have ditched Maggie. I started to worry about her when she ran into Theatre X as everyone was storing the props and bags.

"Olive was here!" I cried.

"Caro! A car T-boned me and drove away! I called Jane. I am so sorry—"

"Maggie!" Jane yelled. She came in wearing black and white checkered pajama pants, a peach hoodie and white Keds. She obviously was relaxing at home. She hugged Maggie then held her at arm's length. "What happened?" Then Jane looked at me and everyone else. "What happened?"

Maggie started. "Someone ran a red light, crashed into me, and took off! A silver Lincoln Continental! Did not get the license! But I'm OK."

"Olive was here!" I said. "She surprised me in the Prop Room. I was alone at the time. She took all the chopsticks, pushed me around, and was ready to do worse when Max showed up. She threatened my family!" I teared up. Damn these emotions! Sally and Max put their arms around me.

Alan and Bill looked puzzled. "A mentally ill woman who I met last year wanted to renew our relationship," I told them. "She startled me, that's all. I'll be fine." I praised their performance and told them they could leave.

"Her parole officer will hear about this," Jane said. She sat down. "Olive and this murder investigation! I need a break in the case and Olive back in custody!"

I suddenly thought about the glove! I needed to tell Jane. I had it in a zip lock baggie in my purse. "Jane, I have to talk to you. Max and Sally, you can go. I'll be fine here. Jane can walk me the short distance to my car."

"Mom! But—" Max said.

Sally abruptly pushed me behind the back curtains. "I have something for you!"

"Can it wait?"

"I don't think so, if you know what I mean!" She took a bottle out of her pocket. "Start taking these pills now. They will start your period."

Murder at Theatre X

"Dragon Pills? Start my period? What?"

"Lower your voice! I am trying to help you! Time is of the essence!"

"I'm not taking any weird herb. I don't like to swallow pills! I—"

"It works, Sister!" We walked back on the stage.

"Lights were perfect!" I said hoping the others would think that's what she wanted to talk about. I stuffed the bottle in my pocket.

"Come on, Max," Sally said. "I'll drive you home."

Max gave me a big hug. I vowed that I will kill Olive myself if she ever hurt one hair on his head.

They left.

"What do you want to talk about, Caro?" Jane asked.

Christina Squire

Chapter 68

Jane and I sat down. Maggie kept standing. She took out her phone.

"Do you mind if Maggie stays?" Jane asked.

"Not at all." Maggie put her phone away and sat. "I found a pair of Nitrile gloves in the Chair's office drawer. God help me, but I took one, and it probably cannot be used in evidence, because there was no search warrant—"

"OK...,and?"

"Well! Clarence told me that Louise's husband had cancer and was at home under Hospice care. Frank must be given fentanyl for the pain. And Professor Smith was poisoned with fentanyl."

Jane looked at me.

"And the professor introduced her husband Frank to Brianne, and Frank left Louise!"

Silence. Why no reaction, I thought?

But I soldiered on: "And the Professor taunted Louise with intimate information about her marriage

231

that Frank had told Brianne and that Brianne then told Richard."

Jane listened.

"Sounds like a movie on the Lifetime channel," Maggie said.

"Life imitates art!" I said to her so happy to have a reaction to this potboiler information. "And the Professor wanted to merge the Cinematic Arts and Theatre Departments, head them both, and control all productions and curriculum! Louise fought that."

Silence.

"She had a motive!" I dramatically pulled the plastic baggie with the glove out of my purse. "I put on a pair of Nitrile gloves before I picked it up," I said proudly.

Jane looked at it. "Good work, Caro, but you're right. We can't use it. But I will check out her alibi again. She certainly does have a strong motive. Thank you." She put the glove in her fanny pack.

"And I thought this was such a major find!"

"Olive had a prescription for fentanyl, too, for her shattered wrist," Jane said.

"Damn! I always thought so. And we found her chopstick in the prop room. But why would Olive want to kill Professor Smith? Then cut off his head?"

"Being a good sister to his ex-wife Marnie? Olive is extremely loyal to her family. We already knew that she killed to protect her husband."

"Protect her own interests, rather!"

Maggie got up. "I'm going to the SUB. Does anyone want coffee?"

We did.

Murder at Theatre X

Jane said, "I interviewed Marnie and Richard's two sons when they flew in from Washington after the murder. The young men had not contacted their mother or answered any of her desperate calls during the long divorce proceedings. Richard said that he would disinherit them if they had anything to do with their mother. Marnie started mixing alcohol and drugs. She almost died of an overdose. Their father never told them."

"Cruelest man! But why did his sons obey him? Oh if that happened to me!" I started to cry.

"Caro! Stop going straight to catastrophe!" She handed me some tissues from her pack. "And if your other two sons have Max's spirit, they will laugh in your husband's face!"

I blew my nose. "I am so emotional lately. Thank you."

"You and James…"

"What about James?"

"He is emotional, too, dealing with some life altering news."

"Something wrong with his daughter Claire?"

"No, thank goodness, but—"

I jumped up. "Why doesn't he ever tell me anything?"

"He feels like you have enough on your mind—"

"What mind? I have no mind!"

"You are so dramatic. Calm down!"

"I care! I do, Jane!"

"He knows that, Caro, with all of his heart."

I held her hand. "Tell me, please."

"What do you want to know, Caro?" James asked.

Christina Squire

Chapter 69

His hair was wet. He wore loose cotton gray pants, white Loyola tee shirt, and black Vans.

"Where have you been?" I asked.

"Swimming. I just read Jane's text. Olive was here?"

"She pushed me down and threatened my family! She ran off with the chopsticks. Someone crashed into Maggie's car. But rehearsal went well! A theatrical evening all around. Sorry you missed it."

Maggie came in with coffees. "Hi, James."

"Glad you're OK, Maggie."

"We've got to go," Jane said. She gave James a look. What did that mean, I thought. Both of them had their little communication signals going. I guess that came from being partners so long. Her look probably meant "Caro is living on the edge". I did not want pity.

"Why do you confide in Jane and not me?" I asked when they left.

"What do you want to know?"

I snapped at his calm demeanor. "Never mind!" I yelled. I started to cry. "I'll try not to know! I will live in a cloud of unknowing!" I took a gulp of coffee. Some spilled out of the cover and dripped down my chin. My stomach cramped. I held the cup out in front of me. I couldn't even stand the smell. "And coffee is making me sick!" I was hysterical! I was cracking up.

James quickly took the cup out of my hand, placed it down on a chair, took me in his arms with such force that the breath was knocked out of me. I struggled. He held me tight. My body went limp. I touched his wet hair and smelled chlorine, put my head on his shoulder and took ragged breaths in between sobs.

He rubbed my back. "So John, Olive and now coffee make you sick?"

"Yes, yes James. They do."

"You have quite a condition..."

"I'm afraid so, James," I said into his neck.

"Everything is going to be all right. Can we go in Professor Block's office?"

James picked up my bag, took the keys out, turned out the theatre lights, and secured the main doors. I followed him like a somnambulist to Sam's office. Dear, patient Professor Block. It was a pleasure to be his graduate assistant.

James unlocked the door. He turned the desk lamp on low. He moved all Sam's files and books off the lumpy purple couch. He took Sam's sweater draped over the back of the desk chair, rolled it up into a pillow, laid me down on the couch, and took off my shoes. He sat down at the end and put my feet in his lap. "Breathe," he said.

He started texting.

I breathed: In through my nose and out through my mouth: Lamaze childbirth training. Glad I still remembered. We were silent a long time. I felt all tension leave my body. He put down his phone. We just looked at each other. He held my feet.

"My commanding officer in New Orleans Chief Montpassent is Olive's uncle," James finally said.

"Her tentacles reach everywhere," I whispered.

"The District Attorney is looking into any ties he had to the Mississippi River drug trafficking."

"What you were investigating when someone tried to kill you and shot your wife Jacqueline."

"Records show that Montpassent has been in contact with his niece Olive. He seeks revenge for me leading the investigation that stopped millions of dollars of drug trade. And his hush money. She will finish the job."

I sat up and tucked my feet under his thigh. "It's almost like she wanted you to come into her sphere again to solve another murder! Like a spider catching you in her web!"

"Not going to happen. Olive has broken her parole threatening you. She'll be back in prison."

"If they find her," I said.

"Maggie's driving Jane's car and looking for Olive now." James sighed. "And…My wife Monique has filed for divorce."

"She woke up?"

"She's very awake with her therapist in Venice."

"Oh James! Is this the same therapist from New Orleans who she ran away with last year?"

"Yes."

237

"Well, I hope he can keep her in a conscious state."

"Then he'll be a better man than I." James laughed.

"Inconceivable," I said. "You all right?"

James stood up. "Monique and I haven't had a real marriage for years. I paid the sanitarium bills. She slept. But she must have had a few lucid moments that I never knew about."

"Just a few."

"You need to go home and get some rest," James said and helped me off the couch. "And don't worry. I ordered a 24 hour police surveillance on your house."

The bottle of Dragon Pills fell out of my pocket and rolled across the floor. James picked it up.

"Dragon Pills?" he asked.

"One of Sally's herbal remedies for fatigue. She gave it to me tonight. You know what a true believer she is in natural medicines." I reached for the bottle. James read the label then handed it to me.

"Fatigue, huh?"

"Oh yeah. I'm fatigued. Horribly."

"I don't want you taking those, Caro. Just stay in bed for a few days," James said.

"As if I have time!"

He walked me to my car. We kissed good-bye. Passionately. I stroked his thick hair. It was still damp. My body felt warm, safe and calm pressed against his. I was convinced for the moment that all was going to be well no matter what the future may hold.

"Don't take that herb," James whispered.

"Never," I said.

Murder at Theatre X

James watched as I backed out of the parking space. I put down the window.

"I'd like to go swimming with you again, James."

"I'd like to go swimming with you again, Caro."

I had a hot flash.

Christina Squire

Chapter 70

I woke up the next day. Ok. I had had it! I was boring myself. Always a dangerous state. Overweight, fright night hair, worrying, hurling, wondering…enough! I decided to skip classes today. My play was going up tomorrow night, and I was going to get a haircut, go to my favorite park, and move through water. Too much reality lately. I needed to step into a dream.

I called Steven's Family Hair Care for an appointment and left a message. Who knows when Steven will come to work. He went to the tune of his own drummer, but I was crazy about his unique vibe. I forgot everything in my life when I was with him. He was wonderfully odd. His salon was like another world. And I liked his thighs.

My breakfast of tea, banana, yogurt and toast agreed with me. I seemed to be over the crud. Or over my nerves. Or over a certain stage. But I refused to think about that! I took Suki for a walk for the first time in weeks. She was so happy, and so was I. We entered Hidden Park, my refuge, through the vine covered narrow alley. Here was the place where I imagined I was dreaming: green grass, beautiful trees, bordered on all sides by fenced back yards, little benches---like a little piece of paradise in the midst of a city. We walked around the park three times. So quiet. The leaves of the trees were rustling. Music to my ears. I was refreshed.

Steven texted that I could come right over. I drove to his house where he cut hair in a garage addition. His car wasn't there, of course. He probably forgot, I thought, but I wasn't upset because that was the way he was. I sat in my car and looked at the sky. I got so lost in the clouds that I didn't notice his tall shadow next to my car. Steven knocked on a window. He was dressed in black jeans, a black tee, and black Converse. His long Yanni like black hair fluttered in the breeze. He had danced for years and kept that dancer body and fluid movement. I thought he was handsome even though he didn't have a chin. He waved me in. I entered the sliding glass doors, walked past the orange Harley-Davidson motorcycle and drum set. He turned on the soundtrack from *Strictly Ballroom*. *Perhaps, Perhaps, Perhaps* filled the room. I stared lovingly at the familiar lumpy couches, chichi pillows, faded Indian rugs, and stringy crochet afghans. The phone rang. Steven answered it and talked a long time in a low voice: Probably another woman wanting to have his baby. He had his groupies. I sat down and flipped through a year old People magazine. He hung up but then walked to a window and stared. Steven did this a lot. He stopped and stared even when cutting hair. He told me that he was exposed to Agent Orange in Viet Nam. Maybe that was why. I didn't care. He could stare all he wanted to. I just liked being in his space. I felt safe and accepted.

He turned away from the window and snapped a towel on the barber's chair. He was calling me. I sat down. He started moving his hands through my hair. I loved that.

"Short and artistic?" he asked.

"Yes," I sighed.

"Let's shampoo you."

"Where is your assistant?" I asked. He always had a pretty Goth girl who shampooed clients, swept up cut hair, flitted around, sang shrilly, and frequently fell asleep on a couch.

"Zoe? She started her own salon."

"What? How can she handle the responsibility?"

"Well, from what I've heard, she pays her bills by moonlighting as an actress in films."

"Films? Zoe?" I exclaimed. "What kind of films?"

"Films where she can do what she does best."

"Shriek? Sweep? Sleep?"

Steven stepped back and stuck out his hip. "Caro, use your imagination."

"Porn?"

"Now called adult entertainment. When Zoe came to pick up her last check, she told me about her latest project. Seems like a friend of her mother's, an old tall thin guy with a greasy comb over brought her a screenplay he had written: a riff on *Beauty and the Beast* and wanted to be cast in the lead. Zoe agreed to play opposite him. But she was traumatized. This guy changed the script during production to be more like *Last Tango in Paris*."

"Did it involve butter--?" I stopped talking when

Steven sprayed my entire head with water getting some up my nose.

Steven squeezed soap in his hand right front of my face. "She said that he brought his own soft spread." He smirked.

"Eeew!" I said. I remembered the scene in the movie where the actor played by Marlon Brando smeared butter on the actress before having vivid, violent sex with her.

Zoe. Unusual name, I thought, as he lathered up my hair. But I had heard it somewhere before.

I closed my eyes to block out all thought.

But...perhaps, perhaps, perhaps?

Chapter 71

My next stop was the Olympic sized indoor swimming pool at the University Johnson Center. I had loved this pool for years and had brought my boys here to swim when they were young. So clean. So big. Huge bay doors opened in warm weather for swimmers to sun on lush, thick grass. Heaven.

I changed into my swimming suit in the locker room and headed for the obligatory showers. I unfortunately looked at myself in a mirror and was shocked out of my dream state. I refused to think about this Rubenesque development! I showered, walked down a hallway to the pool, dove into a lap lane, and felt alive.

My mind cleared. All I did was feel the cool water caressing every inch of my body. I felt the gentle force of the water. I felt my muscles reaching and expanding. I felt whole and strong.

While gliding slowly along with a backstroke I started thinking about Professor Smith's murder. So many suspects! Everyone had a motive! But everyone had an alibi that night. Olive, her mother and sister Marnie were at a movie. But they could have gone out the back exit. And Olive's chopstick was discovered in the Prop Room where Richard's body was found. Isabel and the guitarists Vincente and Joaquin practiced in Carlisle Gym. And the search warrant on their property did not turn up any evidence. The note found with Richard's head was written in Spanish, but Marnie, Olive's sister, was fluent in Spanish. Louise was at a cast party. Both she and Olive had access to fentanyl: Louise because of her husband Frank's cancer and Olive for her wretched wrist. I had yet to hear about what was on the gloves I found in Louise's desk. And actually, Frank was still living with Brianne, the Fox, when he was first diagnosed and may have had a prescription filled while he lived with her, but Brianne was having her hair done at her daughter's salon---

Her daughter Zoe's salon! That's where I had heard that name before, when Jane was listing everyone's alibis! Just who was her mother's tall friend with a comb over who brought his own soft spread? Was he Professor Richard Smith who edited Isabel's beautiful flamenco film into X rated material? Had to be! Did Brianne find out what Richard did to her daughter? I suddenly sank and swallowed a mouthful of water. I kicked and bounced up coughing and sputtering. I saw the lifeguard stand out of her chair. I raised a thumbs up. No more leisurely back stroke! I swam a powerful crawl to the end of the lap lane. I hauled my sturdy body up and out, grabbed my towel off the bench, and walked quickly to the locker room.

Chapter 72

I had to contact my Inspector immediately! I left the locker room without drying or combing my hair, removing the dripping mascara under my eyes or even taking off my bathing suit. I just pulled my pants on over it and threw a towel around my shoulders. I was in the Jonson Center lobby composing an explosive text when I saw him and Jane holding yoga mats under their arms. How sweet was that? Too bad I was about to shatter their *chi*.

"Hey!" I yelled.

They turned around. Speechless.

"I need to talk to you! I discovered some very important information."

"Caro, we'll wait if you want to go back and get dressed," Jane said.

"No! Can't wait! Brianne's daughter Zoe has a beauty salon where she produced X rated movies! I heard that she was in one with a man who resembled Professor Richards where he abused her horribly!"

"Let's get out of here," my Inspector said.

"We can go to my office," Jane said. Then looked at me. "You can use the bathroom there."

247

We half trotted half ran our way down the steps past the Kiva. James took the wet towel off my shoulders and gave me his sweatshirt. "Are you feeling better?" he asked.

"Yes," I said. We turned right on a curved sidewalk.

"Good," he said. "So where did you hear this?" he asked.

"Steven! Steven's Family Hair Care! I was getting a haircut. I asked where his assistant Zoe was. He said that she left to start her own salon, but that she had a side business of producing and acting in adult entertainment. She told Steven about a traumatizing filming experience when she came to pick up a paycheck. This monster used butter on her!"

They both stopped suddenly and looked at me.

"Then I remembered that Brianne's alibi was that she was getting a treatment at her daughter Zoe's salon. Had to be the same Zoe. But I bet she already knew about Zoe's horrible experience before Professor Smith was killed!" I said.

"Brianne had to know before then," Jane said. "She had sent a man who was her friend to her daughter. Zoe would have told her about the full catastrophe immediately."

We continued at a fast clip through a courtyard and entered Hokona Hall: one of the original university dormitories built in the fifties.

I could not stop talking. "And what about the gloves I found in Louise's drawer?"

We walked through dark, gray industrial hallways. "We found traces of fentanyl," Jane said.

"Yes! But what about fingerprints?"

Jane unlocked her office. "We haven't checked for those yet," she said. "It's a complicated process finger-printing latex gloves...We do have Louise's on file."

"Don't assume they are Louise's!" I said. "Brianne had access to fentanyl, because Louise's husband still lived with her when he got diagnosed with cancer. Clarence told me. And she would go to any means to frame Louise. She hated her!"

James took out his phone. "Yes...Inspector Hutchinson here. I want Brianne Morgan brought in. Yes. No, I don't know her address."

"But the Dean of Students will have it," I said. "Or Clarence. And she may be in class now." Do I have to think of everything?

James repeated my suggestions. "And go in the evidence room, get the nitrile gloves and have them checked for fingerprints ASAP. And get a search warrant for Brianne's house." He rang off. "We'll get that lab process going."

I was so relieved but seemed to lose all energy and collapsed in a chair.

"Caro, don't you want to get out of your wet swim suit?" Jane asked.

"I'm good." I took a deep breath, sighed and looked around Jane's office. The walls were painted a light sea green. An Impressionist painting of a woman holding a bouquet of flowers and an oil of gondolas in Venice hung on the wall along with a print of women bull-leaping in Minoan Crete. Interesting combination, I thought. On her desk was a framed photograph of her and Maggie standing at what looked like at the edge of the Grand Canyon.

Jane looked at my crumpled heap of a body. "I'll go to the lounge and get us some coffee."

James placed a chair in front of me and sat. He inched it closer until our knees touched. He took my hands and kissed them. "How are you, Caro?"

"Tired but excited to share this news."

"Excellent work. You are a good investigator. And people talk to you."

"I like to talk."

I looked into his beautiful green eyes. I had spent a day living a dream…until I started thinking. But my thoughts led to an important discovery. I was a good investigator. But I wished I could find some answers in his gaze. And discover how he really felt about me. Only when locked in his passionate embrace was I truly sure of him. Maybe that was enough for now.

James squinted his eyes. "What are you thinking about?"

I squinted mine. "A mystery."

"Can I help you solve it?"

"I certainly hope so."

Chapter 73

I got home and made my mother's recipe for spaghetti and meatballs. It felt so good to cook again. I missed these normal day activities I used to take for granted. I put KUNM on the radio, listened to world music and happily mashed hamburger meat, egg, bread crumbs, parmesan cheese and spices together with my bare hands. I made a dozen meatballs, tossed them in hot olive oil, and rolled them around until browned all over. Douglas and Max were thrilled to come home and smell the marinara sauce bubbling on the stove.

"Mom!" they both exclaimed. "Food! Thank you!" They put their arms around me. This was happiness. I forgot all about murder. I forgot that the Beckett play was opening the next night. I loved my children. I was thankful that I was hungry.

I did not miss John.

I made a big salad. Douglas bought a French baguette at the Coop bakery. I lit a candle. We ate around the red kitchen table.

My phone rang as were finishing. Face Time request from Peter in Austin. I accepted. The handsome face of my *numero uno* lit up the screen.

"What happened?" I yelled.

"Mom! I told you and told you not to yell at the phone! I'm fine! How are you?"

"Great! Your brothers and I just ate dinner!" I held the phone out toward them. Max smiled with a meatball between his front teeth. Douglas tapped a rhythm on glasses with a fork. I went out on the deck.

"So what's up, honey?" I asked.

"Have you looked on line at the *New Orleans Pecayune* newspaper?"

"No."

"Major investigation of the police department, Mom! Chief Montpassent was charged with past involvement in the Mississippi River drug running crime ring. Authorities confiscated his department and home computers. He had received thousands of dollars in kick-backs from the operation and covered up evidence. He is ruined."

"Inspector Hutchinson was right!"

Peter turned to his laptop. He scrolled up.

"And, Mom, the report discovered e-mails sent to a niece, an Olive Walters, a woman accused of murder in Albuquerque, New Mexico! And, Mom, the e-mails from each discussed a James Hutchinson at length: where he lived, who he saw, who he worked with, his daughter Claire! The article went on to give a history of the former New Orleans inspector, the shooting, the unsolved death of his wife, the false accusations of planting evidence…and that he was now working for the Albuquerque Police Department."

Suki was whining at the door. I got up to let her out.

"Was it Montpassent who tried to murder James for getting too close to the truth but killed his wife instead?" I asked.

"They have his guns and are checking ballistics."

"Oh Peter! Justice at last! I hope!"

"Please be careful, Mom! The article said that Mrs. Walters was out on bail. She is dangerous. You may be in her sight lines when she tries to finish the job her uncle started."

"Don't I know it. But Olive is missing now. James ordered a watch on our house. The police are looking for her."

Silence.

"How's Dad?"

Suddenly uncomfortable, I stood up to go inside. "I don't know."

"You don't know?"

"I don't know, Brother!" Why did I feel like I had to explain myself! If Peter wanted to know everything, he should move back here!

Silence.

"I'll call him," Peter said.

"Good."

Christina Squire

Chapter 74

I took a lobster bath. I washed all the chlorine off my skin. I sunk into the tub to soak my head. Then I lathered up my hair, submerged again, took the plug out, and rinsed off with fresh water. I felt so good. And I had such hope that justice will finally come for James and his daughter.

I put on boxer shorts and wife beater tee. I went into the kitchen, opened up the frig, and took out a bottle of white wine. I remembered my well-fed figure. I put it back and filled the teapot with water.

I got blissfully under the sheets with a big cup of chamomile tea and my dog. Douglas was at a rehearsal, and Max said that he was part of a discernment group at church to discuss the hiring of a new youth leader. He told me that many parents had complained that the current youth club activities had nothing to do with Holy Scripture. Max strongly disagreed but agreed to pray about it.

I bet he will.

Tomorrow will be a full day and night. I should study something but instead started to read Kate Atkinson's

Started Early, Took My Dog. My sense of wellbeing was complete.

My phone pinged with a text from James: "Outside. Can I see you? Late. Sorry."

I pulled on floral pajama pants and a sweat shirt. Suki came to my side at the door. I looked through the window. James.

"Brianne confessed to poisoning Richard with fentanyl," he said when I let him in.

"What?"

He bent to pet Suki, then he lifted me up and tried to twirl me around, but I slid, shrieking, down his body to the floor mid whirl. "Thank you for the lead, Caro."

"Well, thanks to Steven and Clarence!"

"No, you." We stood with our arms around each other.

"Ok...if you insist. Now tell me everything."

We sat on the living room sofa. "We got a search warrant for Brianne's house. We found the Professor's cell phone," James said.

"Wow."

"We told Brianne that we found her fingerprints on the nitrile gloves in Louise's drawer."

"What did she say?" I asked.

"Nothing."

"Nothing?"

"But when Jane pulled up a video on the professor's phone of the movie he made with her daughter, Brianne collapsed."

"Horrible."

"She started screaming that he deserved to die! She smeared fentanyl on his face wearing the gloves. Frank,

Louise's husband, had left some at her house when he moved out."

"Oh!"

"She begged us not to prosecute her daughter who was just trying to protect her by providing an alibi. Brianne said that Zoe had suffered enough."

"I'll say...but Brianne made such a scene when he was beheaded."

"She was as surprised as anyone, Caro. And she is in the Dramatic Writing Program."

"There's that..."

"She did not cut off his head. She swore. But she was so glad somebody did. He could not die too many times after what he did to her daughter."

"Hmmm...coffee?

"Yes." Who wants to sleep? Suki jumped up next to him.

"Are you hungry?" I yelled from the kitchen. "I have some left-over spaghetti!"

"Love some," he said.

I heated up a bowl full in the microwave, sliced the extra baguette, and spread it with butter. I sprinkled freshly grated Parmesan cheese on the spaghetti. I served the food to my Inspector on a tray the Macedonian way. He was so happy.

I brought our coffees in and sat down on the couch with the dog between us. Suki and I watched James eat with great interest.

"Delicious," he said when finished. "Thank you, Caro."

"Welcome," I said and lightly kissed him. He pulled me close. Suki jumped down. He gave me a proper

Christina Squire

kiss. Warmth spread throughout my body. I could not help it. Will this feeling ever end?

Chapter 75

After some delightful kissing and such, we ended up with my head in his lap, my legs flung over the top of the couch, and his stocking feet up on the coffee table. I held his hand over my heart. I wondered if he had heard about the news from New Orleans. I hesitated to bring it up in case he got agitated again. I did not feel like this was good time. But maybe I better say something---

"Who cut off his head after he was dead?" James asked.

Thank goodness! We could talk about this murder. "Someone else who hated him intensely," I said. "And who maybe wanted to throw suspicion on the guitarists from Mexico because the beheadings south of the border are splashed all over the news. And leaving a note in Spanish."

"Vincente and Joaquin were very upset about what happened to Isabel."

"True." I sat up. "James! Maybe, just maybe the person who cut off his head did not know he was already dead!"

259

"Explain."

"Well! I read *A Nest of Vipers*—"

"By Andreas Camilieri?"

"Yes! Have you read it?"

"Not that one."

"Well! Inspector Montalbano had to solve quite a puzzle. An elderly man was found dead of a gunshot wound sitting at his kitchen table with an empty coffee cup in front of him. The Inspector thought he was looking for one murderer until the autopsy reports came in. Turns out the man's coffee was poisoned! He died and slumped over the table. Another character came in later, saw what looked like the man asleep at the table, and shot him in the head!"

"So you're saying that someone could have come into the Professor's office, thought he was asleep instead of in a deadly fentanyl coma, and chopped off his head?"

"Yes."

"We've never found that murder weapon. We know it was not an ordinary butcher knife. It had a serrated edge. Like a saw."

"A tool. From a garage!"

Suki hopped back up on the couch and resumed her place between us. As it should be.

"Have you checked with Robert Hale to see if any of his saws are missing?"

"The man who found the body?"

"Yes. He is the Set Design professor. His lab is a large as an airplane hangar. A worker man's heaven of a garage."

"Someone had to have a master key to get in there, Caro."

260

Murder at Theatre X

As our conversation grew more animated Suki leaned back and put her paw on James's shoulder. He scratched her chest.

"All the professors, the chair, and Clarence have one. Students and accompanists don't. I mean, I had to get separate keys to separate doors. But James! Olive must have had a key to get into the prop room. We know she was in there. Her sister Marnie must have her husband Richard's keys. They've never been found."

James started texting. "Jane and I will meet with Robert Hale tomorrow."

"Well! I'm busy tomorrow. My show is opening! Are you coming?"

"I certainly hope so."

Suki jumped off the couch.

Christina Squire

Chapter 76

The big day arrived. I was more nervous directing than if I were acting in a play. Thank goodness it was a short piece. And my actors were good and my sister and Max were my best boys. But later I had to show up for academic classes without finished assignments and plead for mercy. But this was the Theatre Department! It was not like I was at the beach. They should understand. I will block out next week for schoolwork, period.

Unless there was an interesting development in the professor's murder.

I could not do everything!

I dressed appropriately in Beckett mode: black pants (Did I shrink them?), black long-sleeved tee, and black boots. I ate a light breakfast of Cheerios and a banana. My stomach was churning. Maybe it was because the kitchen smelled on the spaghetti Max must have eaten before school. I thought about smoking on the deck to calm down, but the thought nauseated me. I guess this was a positive body reaction. I was proud of myself. And a little concerned. But I could not think about that now!

263

Posters for the play had been up a week. Students and professors saw me in the hall and said they were coming. Clarence was coming ("Wouldn't miss those gorgeous guys coming out of a bag.") Isabel came in the office to pick up mail for the Dance Program while I was there. She gave me a big hug and whispered *buena suerte* in my ear. Even Louise came out of her office, said 'break a leg' and patted me on the back. I realized for all the clashing egos and scrambling for attention most everyone here supported their fellow artists. For the first time I felt happy to be part of this dramatic family. I was excited. I felt alive.

Curtain was 7:30. Everyone was meeting at 6:30. I checked all my props. It was only 5:00. I should get something to eat.

I sat in a booth facing Central Avenue at the Frontier Restaurant. I watched a live reality show as I ate a grilled cheese sandwich with a real Coke: couples arguing, people exchanging money/drugs/business cards (?), lovers loving, beggars begging, skateboarders and bike riders weaving through the crowded sidewalk, dog walkers and someone with a goat on a leash. Central was filled with bumper to bumper rush hour traffic. Did I see a silver Lincoln Continental go by? I got a chill. How many Lincolns were there in Albuquerque? And Olive probably ditched hers. I could not think about that woman now.

My sister texted me: *Where r u?* Sally soon joined me with a half-sized vegetarian salad. She brought her own thermos of green tea.

"I can't believe how you devour movie theatre hot dogs and Diet Cokes and eat clean every other day."

Murder at Theatre X

"Moderation in all things," she said and sipped her tea. "So how are you, Caro?"

"Nervous!"

"No..." She chewed a slice of hard-boiled egg. "How ARE you?"

"I think fine. I just can't smoke anymore."

"Thank goodness...Any...developments?"

"No. And I can't think about this right now, Sally!"

"I have a test in my purse."

"Did you hear me?" My phone pinged. Text from Max: *sick! hurling! sorry!*

"Max caught my flu, Sally!"

"Did he? Hmmm...Poor baby." She put the pregnancy test in my purse.

I texted my Inspector. He replied immediately that he was already in the Fine Arts Building and could operate the goad.

"Let's do this, Sister!" Sally linked arms with me as we crossed Central on our way to Theatre X. The show must go on.

Christina Squire

Chapter 77

I was still arm and arm with my sister walking down the basement hallway to Theatre X when I saw James sprinting towards us. We broke apart as if to brace ourselves. He held my upper arms. I thought he was going to start shaking me. His eyes were brighter green. His hair stood on end.

"Caro! The forensic team was in the design lab all day. They turned a UV Light on all the saws and found bone fragments between the teeth of one."

"Oh!" I exclaimed. "Can they test it to see if it's the Professor's?"

"It's being tested now…once again you came up with the best clue. Hell with theatre. Join the police force!" He hugged me.

"Plenty of drama there, too!" I laughed.

James turned to Sally. "Your sister is amazing."

"I've always thought so," she said. "And I am glad to hear that you think so, too." She stared at him.

His smile faded.

"Well! Beckett calls!" I said after a few awkward seconds. Sally better back off! I did not need her in full Tiger Sister mode. Not now at least.

267

We went into Theatre X by the main door. A second door down the hall was used by actors who had to exit stage left. They then could walk down the hall and go through the main door if they have an entrance stage right. I requested a proscenium arrangement of the chairs. Everyone sat the same way facing the action. Black curtains hung on the right and left sides of the theatre.

Bill and Alan were doing yoga poses on the floor.

"Hi, guys! Good to stretch out. Will help getting in and out of those bags."

"We're ready, Caro! How are you doing?" Alan asked.

"Nervous but so glad to have you both in this play. You're great!"

"Don't worry, Caro," Bill said. "Namaste." He pressed his palms together and bowed.

"Namaste," I replied, pressed my palms together and bowed to them.

Sally positioned herself behind the stage right curtains at the light. James ran the goad back and forth behind the curtains at stage left. The house was opening in 10 minutes. I heard people talking in the hallway. I took a deep breath.

"OK. Places everyone," I said. Bill and Alan collected their props and got into the sacks. A neat pile of a folded coat and trousers with boots and a hat on top was between them. I checked on Sally and James. Both gave me a thumbs up. I sat down in the center of a middle row. My heart was pounding.

The main door opened. People filed in. I was so glad anyone came! You never knew. Beckett was not exactly

268

Murder at Theatre X

a theatre blockbuster. Louise arrived. And Sam. And Douglas! He gave me a hug and sat beside me. Jane came over, hugged me, too, and sat on my other side.

"Maggie is looking for Olive or she would be here," Jane said.

Clarence moved, hips swaying, between the rows and sat behind me.

He stuck his head between Jane and me. "Where's the bootylicious Inspector?"

"Behind the curtain holding a goad."

"Oooh! Naughty boy!"

Jane laughed. I surprised myself by flushing beet red. Hormones.

Lights went down. Pitch black. Then a low, bright beam of light shone over two bags.

I heard a door open and close. Latecomers! But the ushers locked the main door when show started. I looked back to where the stage left door was located behind the curtains. The fabric waved back and forth. I thought I heard the shuffling of feet. Nerves.

269

Christina Squire

Chapter 78

The show went well. The audience was so responsive. They laughed at Alan and Bill chewing carrots, brushing their teeth, and all their pantomimes and expressions of sadness or perkiness living life in a bag. I was so proud of them. They even often laughed when the goad wheeled out. But James must have forgotten how many times to prod the bags. The goad poked again and again instead of once. The audience did not know the difference, but I wondered why. The goad was supposed to be subtle not aggressive. Something was not right. My stomach turned over.

The audience clapped and hooted when Alan and Bill crawled out of their sacks to take a bow. The actors turned, faced toward my sister and clapped. Sally came out and took a bow. The audience applauded. The three of them looked toward James and clapped. No James. Some in the crowd stamped their feet to call him out. There was a lot of noise.

A chill went through me. I grabbed Jane's hand. She gave me a look before stepping over people's feet to run down to the stage. I followed her.

"Mom! Be careful!" Douglas yelled. "I'm coming with you!"

"So am I, Girlfriend!" Clarence called.

The four of us joined my sister staring dumbly at the goad on the floor. I looked down the dark narrow passage between the curtains and the wall. The stage left door was ajar.

"Jane!" I screamed. "Olive got him! She'll kill him!" Douglas put his arms around me.

"I could not see anything!" Sally exclaimed. "The light was too bright!"

Bill and Alan came behind the curtain. "Why are you screaming? What happened?"

"James is missing," Douglas said. "He's in trouble."

"What can we do?" Alan asked.

"Let's search this building," Jane said. "She doesn't have that much of a head start."

Douglas picked up the goad. "Mom, is this the same Olive who was arrested for murder last year and tried to have you killed?"

"Yes," I said. "She is out on parole and has vowed to take revenge on me and James. She's crazy."

"I'll check the rooms in the basement," Clarence said and ran out with Bill and Alan.

While Jane called the police, Maggie ran in out of breath. "I was following a silver Lincoln. I thought Olive was driving. But it was Olive and Marnie's mother wearing a wig, a jumpsuit and long red nails! She led me on a wild goose chase to the Target on Paseo del Norte—"

"You did your best, Maggie, but we have to find them

Murder at Theatre X

now!" Jane said. "The police will watch the roads and search this building and surrounding area."

People were still lingering in the hallway, chatting away. Clarence and the actors pushed their way through them. "I've opened all the classrooms, closets, and dressing rooms in this part of the basement," Clarence said. "Nothing. If Olive has a master key, she could be anywhere. I'll check the next three floors…but you can check out the costume morgue around the corner."

Clarence unlocked the double heavy metal doors and turned on the light. Jane, Clarence, Bill and Alan climbed up the steps out of the basement. Douglas, Sally, Maggie and I went into the morgue.

Christina Squire

Chapter 79

Rows and rows of clothing hung on garment racks in this huge space. I never knew it existed. It went on and on. I thought it even went far under the huge Popejoy Hall stage that was adjacent to Rodey Theatre. There were costumes for every historical age, shoes, hats; a long shelf of wig heads. This place freaked me out. Like I was entering a house of horror. I imagined I even saw some clothes swaying on their hangers. A musty old smell hung in this airless space.

I screamed, "James!"

Silence except for the hissing of the exposed pipes in the ceiling.

We saw abandoned sewing machines, ironing boards, irons, and baskets of ribbons and thread. Then we walked by a row of mannequins.

James was standing at the end.

Olive peeked around him. "Oh hello! You found us!"

"James," I whispered.

"Isn't he handsome?" Olive purred. She stroked his chest from behind. "He could be a manikin in the windows of the best New York City department stores. I think he missed his calling, don't you?"

James stared straight ahead with his arms at his side. I tried to make eye contact with him. He was like a statue: stiff and so still. He was not wearing his blazer. His shirt was wrinkled and hung over of his pants. I saw bloody scratches on his face. Olive slithered around beside him. She put her arm around his shoulders. She was dressed in black, hair done up a big knot on top of her head, face garishly made up with kohl rimmed eyes and thick violet lipstick, and she held a gun in a blood red manicured hand.

We froze.

"Yes, he missed his calling," Olive went on. "Instead of dying in a New Orleans gutter, his pretty wife was killed. My uncle was a bad shot. But I'm not." She aimed the gun at his head. "Not from this distance! James ruined my uncle's career. He brought shame upon my family. And arrested me last year for the murder of a worthless human being!" She laughed. She waved her gun at me. "And you, poor besotted Caro, helped him. And I insisted you both framed me!" She ran the gun down his cheek. "I did love beating that vagrant to death. To protect my then husband, of course. I am family oriented."

"Olive," I sneered. "Avenging angel."

"You better believe it, Caro!"

She kept waving her gun at me, but I kept talking even though my sister squeezed my arm. "Then I'm sure it was a shock when Richard dumped your poor sister for another woman," I said. "Did you know that Richard bragged that he now had a fox in his bed?"

"What did you say?" Olive screamed.

"No more boring Marnie. But a young, sexy, clever, foxy woman. He told everyone."

"Shut up! He was another worthless human being! Richard turned their children against Marnie. She became suicidal!"

"Sad," I said.

"Sad for him!"

"How sad, Olive?"

"Very, very sad. I tried to talk some sense into him. He treated me like I was a crazy—"

"Well…" I sighed.

"I hate you, Caro."

"Now that hurts."

Olive stopped waving the gun and held it steady on me. "Oh, you're going to hurt."

James stepped forward. Olive stuck the gun under his chin. He stepped back. I wondered why he didn't knock the gun out of her hand and choke her. He was like a robot.

"Something had to be done," Olive said and kissed the gun. "Richard ruined my sister's life and insulted me…he underestimated me."

"Now that's a crime," I cooed.

"No one does that to me!" she shouted, eyes wild.

Olive turned to James and touched her lips to his ear. "I heard you were hired here. I was happy." She licked his cheek. "Could we meet again? The possibilities were endless. How could I dispense justice for Marnie and," she yelled, "have you fall right into my lap?"

"That's a cliché, Olive," I stage whispered. Sally elbowed me.

"I don't give a fuck!"

Now, I thought. She was almost there. "Poor Richard," I said. "He loved the fox so much. And her daughter, too..."

"Animal! He was an animal!" Olive shrieked. "He was going to die a long painful death! I swore to God! Of fentanyl poisoning! Yes! He was! His office door was open! The bastard was asleep at his desk. Probably drunk! He always drank too much! I hated his face!" She was spitting saliva with every word and jabbing the gun in James's side. "I had the brilliant idea to cut off his head. The Mexican guitarists would be blamed. That's what people do down there. They hated Richard for what he did to Isabel's film. I'll have Marnie write a note in Spanish---"

"*Ole,*" I said. Sally pinched me.

Olive pointed the gun at me. James leaned forward. Olive put the gun to his temple. "---and I'll stuff him in Caro's bags just for fun! I do have a sense of humor." She took a big ragged breath. "I took Richard's keys and found a saw in the set garage. I called my mother and Marnie to help me lug his guts to the prop room. Marnie got hysterical seeing his head, so I dumped it at the recycling center—"

"Richard was already dead when you cut off his head, you stupid cunt," I said.

Olive stared at me, stunned. Maggie started to move.

"Stop!" Olive screeched. "After I kill James, I'm leaving the country. And you will never follow because—"

My knees buckled. Sally broke my fall. I saw Marnie,

Olive's sister, coming from behind a rack of clothes on my right with Max. His mouth was taped and his hands tied in front of him. She held a gun to his back. We all stood facing Olive and James.

"We are taking Max with us," Olive said. "I'll kill him if followed."

She pointed the gun at James. She cocked the trigger. She smiled.

"No!" I screamed. Sally held me tight.

Max jabbed Marnie's throat with his elbow. She fell to the ground gagging. Maggie kicked the gun out of her hand. It skidded across the floor and hit Olive's foot. Olive looked down. Max lurched forward and head butted her. Olive stumbled backwards, reeling, off balance. James stuck his foot out behind her. She tripped over it and fell on her back. The gun went off. We ducked. A wig head flew off a shelf. Olive wildly aimed at James from the floor but dropped the gun when Douglas stabbed her in the face with the goad. Many times.

"My eyes!" she cried.

James squeezed Olive's throat until she was unconscious with blood streaming from her sockets. Maggie flipped Marnie over on her stomach, sat on her back, pinned her arms behind her with one hand and whipped out her cell phone with the other. "My sister was trying to protect me! She loves me!" Marnie wailed over and over again.

I dropped my purse and ripped the tape off Max's mouth. Sally pulled a Swiss Army knife out of her bag and cut Max free. We both threw our arms around him. Then we hugged Douglas. James crushed me in his embrace. I burst into tears.

"How did your show go, Mom?" Max asked.

Chapter 80

I sat in the huge, soft black leather front seat of the Jeep Commander. James was taking me to his home at Cimino Compound for the first time. The windows were down. The air in the North Valley smelled so good: fresh, clean and green. It was like another city away from brown, dusty Albuquerque. We drove along Rio Grande Boulevard. I admired the houses set far back from the road and watched horses roaming on spacious fenced properties. I even saw a few buffalo.

We passed the Rio Grande Nature Center with its bird refuge and bike and walking paths along the Bosque, the wooded area along the Rio Grande River. Just a few years ago I used to walk there, sit on a rock and stare at the gently flowing water. I was restless and bored. My children were grown. My marriage was comfortably numb. I was bursting with energy and did not know what to do with it. I yearned for something yet unknown.

Now I was not that same woman. I no longer felt like I was a hag without a future. Well, I might be a hag, and a pregnant one at that, but I had a future. I performed with the best of them. I was the one who solved three murders. I felt successful and competent. And ready for more.

And I will have a Master's Degree in Theatre Arts. All the world's a stage after all.

But a baby will change my life. If I was pregnant, I hoped I'd have a girl this time. I was on my way, and she will go with me.

And James? I looked at his handsome profile. Still so mysterious. Still so desirable. Will he be there for his child and me? I did not know. And I did not try to know.

I was still counting on menopause.

And counting…

Chapter 81

"Hold still, James!" I placed a temporary tattoo of a Celtic dragon on his upper arm. I pressed it down with one hand and dipped a sponge in a bowl of warm water with the other. I wet the tattoo thoroughly and pressed firmly. His head was propped up on pillows. His eyes were dreamy. I felt rather dreamy myself, but I was on a mission. "Just 30 seconds," I said.

"Whatever you say."

I peeled off the paper backing. Then I rinsed and smoothed with water. Gently. Then I lay down beside him, held his hand and blew on the red-feathered dragon. "Has to dry," I said.

"Whatever you say."

My phone pinged. It was on his end table next to the condoms. A text from Max: At YMCA with a.Sally. Taekwondo! OX. I showed James. "Now OX means he really wrote the text. After Olive made him text me that he was sick, Max developed this code of authenticity."

"He'll make a good detective someday."

I took a tube of Neosporin off the table and dabbed some on the scratches on his face. James took my hand

Christina Squire

and kissed my inner wrist. I got chills but kept talking. "Well! If Max wants to be a good detective, he needs to develop better sense. He shouldn't have been smoking in the alley behind Hurricane's where Olive kidnapped him. Police surveillance would have seen her go to the house. Not to mention Suki's reaction." I blew on the dragon. "Perfect! Look at the flames coming out of its mouth."

"I'll show you flames," James said. He kissed me. Passionately. White-hot heat shot through me.

Later James picked out a Free-Spirit Purple Butterfly from my booklet of Celtic temporary tattoos. He applied it gently on my left breast. I responded immediately to his light touch. Drops of warm water ran down my body. He blew on the butterfly with soft, slow breaths. I had a moment. I grabbed his hair and moved against him.

"Hold still, Caro," he said smiling.

"Whatever you say...butt."